Appre

"I've been tellii [...]llmark to anyone who will listen. This wonderful book is a testament to the power of humanity and the audacity of spirit. It is a treasure."
- *Steve Farber, Leadership Consultant, Speaker and Author*

"In my 29 years of working with seniors, I've often been inspired by their stories. Stories can change the way we view aging, and the way we view ourselves. Readers of this unique collection will find themselves part of an honest conversation between friends - true accounts of struggles, joys, post-war memories and late loves - that invites them to consider living with more hope, and even with more audacity. It is a true gift from our elders."
- *Paul Klaassen, President, Sunrise Senior Living*

"These heart-felt, poetic stories not only offer glimpses into the lives of the seniors she works with, but the author has made herself vulnerable too, and inevitably the interviews have become conversations between equals. With wonderful artistry, Melody Goetz has shaped what she has gathered into story-gems that find a fitting home in this lovely book. It will be a gift to every reader."
-*Sarah Klassen, Poet, Fiction Writer, & Editor*

"Melody Goetz opens a 'not so small window' on the strengths and challenges of a remarkable group of elders. With sensitivity, empathy and personal engagement, the author embraces the essence of the 'strengths model' in modern gerontology (study of aging). These stories illuminate elders' abilities to continue to contribute to society, and challenge stereotypes. This collection can certainly be used as a supplemental text that stimulates critical thinking in any gerontology course."
- *Pieter Steyn, Professor of Gerontology and Social Work, University of the Fraser Valley*

this small window

Published by Hallmark Communities/Conexions Press
Copyright 2009 by Melody Goetz

All Rights Reserved

Published in Canada by Hallmark Communities Inc./Conexions Press.
#201-32112 South Fraser Way, Abbotsford, BC   V2T 1W4

Printed in Canada

Note: Some of the people in this book have chosen to have their real names used; other stories use pseudonyms. While all these stories are true in essence, some details may be changed to shelter the privacy of individuals within them.

Cover Photo: Melody Goetz

Library and Archives Canada Cataloguing in Publication

Goetz, Melody
This small window : true stories from well-aged people / Melody Goetz.

Includes bibliographical references.
ISBN 978-0-9813507-0-7

1. Older people--British Columbia--Biography. 2. British Columbia--Biography. I. Title.

HQ1060.5.G63 2009   920.0084'609711   C2009-906255-0

Conexions Press
Abbotsford, BC, Canada

Contents

Dedicated, with love, to my parents,
who live their stories
with a faithfulness and vibrancy
that knows no age.

Be kind, for everyone you meet is fighting a great battle.
- *Philo of Alexandria*

All that is gold does not glitter,
Not all who wander are lost.
The old that is strong does not wither,
Deep roots are not reached by the frost.
- *J. R. R. Tolkien*

this small window

true stories from well-aged people

melody goetz

Conexions
PRESS

Foreword

*T*he story of Hallmark Retirement Communities has been quite an adventure. Many have helped shape what it has become today, and have planted the seeds of what it may become tomorrow. Over the years, hundreds of elderly people have walked through the front doors of our two retirement communities into their new homes. For most of us, it takes courage just to think about a move, let alone to do so later in life. I will never forget watching a pickup truck back up to the side door of our first Hallmark, holding apparently all the possessions of a gentleman in the process of making that move. If I live to old age, a simple life will be forced on me if I am not prepared to accept it along the way. I may claim a desire for a simpler life, but not much of my life would back up that claim. If God sees fit for me to live that long, I too may pull up to an eldercare home, perhaps even one of the Hallmarks, and complete a physical move into a new home in less than thirty minutes. I wonder how long it takes for the emotional move to happen.

We started a tradition in our first years of operation called the "Housewarming Luncheon". It's a time for the corporate staff, my wife Grace, and myself to meet new residents and hear a little of their stories. The new resident is encouraged to invite two other guests – perhaps family or friends. We gather around the table in Hallmark's family dining room for a wonderful meal provided by our staff. I begin by proposing a possible agenda for the time together, of course leaving latitude for the unscripted conversations that often develop. I pose a question for each attendee to consider within their response, such as: "Describe the first school that you can remember," or "Tell us about the closest little general store to where you lived." It's an attempt to dispel the inevitable nervousness common to us all when asked to talk about ourselves.

The stories that have unfolded over the years are amazing. We have often wished that we could record them and keep them to be shared freely, as freely as they were given to us during the luncheons.

Melody has now recorded some of those stories fortunately, but more importantly, has spent time with a number of residents, one-on-one, to learn from their lives and hear more of their stories.

These stories perhaps allow the reader to listen in on a sacred conversation. The vulnerability of the elder is matched by the vulnerability of the author, as she muses and plumbs the conversation as it applies to her own life. If we allow ourselves space, we will readily realize that we are all in this together, and that one's experience is often a shared experience. We can learn from these stories that are given back to us as gifts, free for the reading. Perhaps these stories can help us live our lives more fully, more as we were intended to live. Perhaps we can see the value in embracing who we are, and live out our lives from that place, that center. More importantly, perhaps it will also encourage each of us to value the story of our own life.

As Parker Palmer said in *The Active Life*, "the marvellous thing about learning from a story is that a story never ends, so our learning from it need not end either."[1]

Stan Hindmarsh
President, Hallmark Communities, Inc.

Introduction

uite the view, isn't it?" asked Marion, as she came to stand beside me. "I have this small window," she said. "It's like a window in time. Early the other morning, I saw two fellows go by on bicycles that were all hung over with bags. It took me right back to the Depression. So many men were on the move then; there was no work, there was nothing for them." She was quiet for a moment, remembering. "Still, any time is a good time to be alive, even the Depression." We stood together, looking across the billows of dark green trees to the small waterway, alive with ducks and geese.

For over a decade now, I have been working amidst the residents of two Hallmark retirement communities. During this time, I've often toyed with the idea of writing down some of the stories that have come my way. I am a writer, why not pass them on?

As I began my research, going back over a decade's worth of notes and journal entries, the faces and stories of Hallmark's many residents came flooding back. I remembered conversations in people's suites, and in my office, and now wondered: how could I ask a woman who had suffered both the sudden loss of her spouse and her hearing to turn down the volume of her radio? Where had I found the audacity to enter the suite of a concentration camp survivor who'd just been told by another resident that the Holocaust had been "blown out of proportion", or to ask a dame associated with royalty to tone down the strength of her perfume? Thankfully, the demands of my early years as Executive Director had kept me mostly oblivious to the absurdity of my 'leading' these people. I'd begun as a 'halfling' after all, with most of them double my years. And so, with quaking knees and pleas for wisdom, I've done all these things and more. Not because I've always known what I was doing, but because I've been tasked to do the best I can to foster healthy, life-giving community. I've found these well-aged people to be gracious and forthright, patient and not-so-patient, and we've carried on as best we can. Years later, I am in awe that I've been allowed into the lives and stories of so many. And so, I want to collect these words that have been given to me, lift them to the light and remember the life that has been given and lived.

Who am I to try to articulate these stories? Fortunate, I guess; some would say blessed. So many stories go unspoken. I write these stories then, if for no other reason, than to listen, for every one of them has written itself upon me.

I have this small window. Into the lives of these elders I have come to love. Into this life I've been given. Into this astonishing place, this beautiful earth.

Gift of the elders

Edna was my roommate in Guatemala. I had never roomed with an eighty-six year-old before, and was very conscious of her heart condition. For the first few nights, I lay awake, listening for her breathing, and if I didn't hear it, I'd get out of my bed and quietly stand beside hers, my eyes straining to discern her form through the darkness. I'd hold my palm in the air above her face, hoping to feel the reassuring coolness of breath. Needless to say, I didn't sleep so well. As far as I know, however, Edna had fantastic sleeps, so deep she hardly needed to breathe!

One night Edna told me about some of her experiences while raising seven children. She'd done such a great job of it that they didn't need her so much any more, and now, more recently, her husband had died. Just before we turned out the light, she said, "I feel superfluous in the world." That was Edna - ever-eloquent, ever-succinct - even when speaking of something so disquieting. I didn't know what to say. In my relative youth, I couldn't comprehend how that might feel, or how one would endure that kind of life change. I did think, however, "Edna just articulated the cry of elderly people in our culture." I wondered what could bring a much-needed sense of purpose back into the season of aging.

Her suffering spoken, ever-practical Edna wakened each day in Guatemala, dressed, and joined us for breakfast. She was pleasant, committed, and resolute. She played with children in orphanages, visited with Guatemalan elders in a care home, and - when she became tired - uncomplainingly endured bumping along the cobblestone streets in a wheelchair. The children didn't seem to care about her grey hair or her limited mobility; they swarmed Edna in her wheelchair, fighting for a place on her lap, coveting her attention. They had her laughing, and she them; they called her 'Abuela', or 'Abuelita', words meaning 'grandmother', or, more tenderly, 'little grandmother'. Upon her return, when asked to comment on her Guatemalan experience, Edna smiled and said; "Guatemala is the jewel in the crown of my old age."

There had been moments of tenderness between us all - which I so easily forget, or find hard to take in -

but this one so memorable: Edna turned to me and said, "You care for me as though you are my own daughter." My thoughts returned to our earlier conversation, and her underlying question of, 'What do I give now?' Once Edna had been needed by seven children, and now she needed to accept the care of others.

How strange it all is, and not always comforting, that we all must let go of what we know. The givers must learn to receive, the receivers learn to give. In the end, is it all the same somehow, do these opposites come together, and make life whole?

I write these stories for the Ednas of this world, for the many elders whose stories and lives are vivid and real, the telling of which can enrich and fill those of us with many years still to live. These elders have graciously lived – survived – the hard lessons, and now face what may be the most difficult adventure of all: the rocky and heartbreaking terrain of letting go, in trust. From the crucible of that journey, they pass on a rich inheritance to those of us approaching from behind. Far from being superfluous in the world, they are relevant and essential. Their stories are the gift of the elders to their children, their children's children, and the world they love. Our history, our roots, our bedrock.

Finding the way home

euben came to our community with a history full of romance, the romance of gold panning in northern British Columbia in the early 1900's. It was rumoured that Reuben was one of the few that had struck it rich. His past may also have included a woman who couldn't handle northern life – or was it life with 'northern Reuben'? Reuben came to us wearing beige and brown checked fortrel pants, hiked up well above his waist and cinched tight to his thin torso with a worn black belt. Reuben was a bit of a wild thing – he looked like a Gold Rush veteran – what with his thick hair that stuck out straight, dark as an old rubber tire, and his jet black eyes, always snapping and ready for something. Reuben sometimes forgot his teeth. Reuben sometimes forgot where he was. Sometimes Reuben even forgot his closest friend's name – but Jake did not forget him.

Jake was an old wartime buddy of Reuben's, more than willing to tell anyone the story of how Reuben had saved his life, and how he was forever in his debt. Jake's actions proved him faithful; he was in the building with Reuben more often than not, helping Reuben find his way down the halls and to the dining room. He knew Reuben's ways and habits better than Reuben himself.

Reuben's fading memory was of some concern, as were his wandering behaviours – in Assisted Living, everyone is free to come and go as they please, unmonitored. Could the safety net of our community provide what Reuben needed to flourish without compromising his safety? Jake was persuasive; the wandering behaviours, he was convinced, would lessen when Reuben felt more at home – he would eventually find his way. Meanwhile, Jake was willing to bear the risk on behalf of his friend. "Reuben is a free spirit," Jake told us, as if we hadn't noticed. "He would die if he was locked up."

And so, Reuben became part of our community. Everyone kept an eye out for him, and when he seemed unsure about where he was headed, someone would be on hand to help him find his way. Still, with the passage of time, it seemed Reuben's disorientation remained unaltered; simply put, he seemed like a fish out of water.

One early evening, my home phone rang, and the Concierge on the other end said, in a rather panicky voice, "Reuben's gone – we don't know where he is."

When I arrived at Hallmark, a police cruiser was parked near the entrance. The building had already been searched, including Reuben's room. All that was known was this – that Reuben was gone, that he was wearing his favourite fortrel pants, and that he'd forgotten his wallet and his teeth on his bed. He was last seen at breakfast – and it was not until late in the afternoon, when a staff member went to his room to remind him to take his medication, that Reuben was missed.

We organized teams of searchers – one to once again search the building, another to go door-to-door in the immediate neighbourhood, and yet another to walk through the park adjacent to Hallmark. I joined the team searching the park. As we walked alongside the small stream amidst the trees, peering into the brown muddy water, there was a chill silence among us - for this would be the unthinkable, one of our greatest fears. Our search took place in fall, and darkness fell early. While we were relieved that the small cold beams of our flashlights did not reveal anything, that relief was short-lived, for when we returned to the building, there was still no sign of Reuben.

Meanwhile, Reuben's friend Jake had arrived. He'd brought us a recent, somewhat blurry photo of

Reuben, which we photocopied and gave to the police and the searchers. Through the open window of his big 4-wheel-drive northern truck, thick fingers tight on the steering wheel, Jake listened carefully to our description of the places we'd searched. We speculated together. He suggested finally that there was a slim possibility that Reuben may have simply gone back home. "Where was home?" we asked. It turned out that Reuben had lived for the better part of a decade in a small apartment building in Vancouver, and had gotten to know the territory like the back of his hand – as well, no doubt, as he'd known every bend of shoreline along his claim during the Gold Rush.

"But how would he get there?" we all wondered; his wallet was up in his room, and money is needed to travel from Abbotsford to Vancouver. "Try the bus depot anyway," said Jake, and we did. The police delivered Reuben's photograph to the bus depot, as well as to local taxi offices, and staff who had worked the earlier shift were contacted. The rather colourful description of an elderly man with checked fortrel pants and no teeth was bound to jog someone's memory. One taxi driver recognized our description of Reuben. He said Reuben had flagged him down somewhere on Princess Street, and had asked him to drive him to the bus depot.

Jake drove back home, found Reuben's previous landlord's phone number, and called him. The landlord had seen no sign of him. We asked him to keep his eyes open, and gave him our phone number. Now what? By now it was eight p.m., and very dark. We walked the park once more.

It seemed a long night awaited us. Then, at 9:30 pm, we received a phone call from Vancouver. It was Reuben's landlord. As he was preparing for bed, he'd looked outside his window – and there was Reuben, sitting quietly on the bench at the bus stop in front of the building waiting for someone to open the front door. The landlord let him in, gave him something to eat, and called us.

Jake picked up his unprotesting friend in his big northern truck, and as they roared down the highway back to Abbotsford, Jake pieced together the story. Indeed, Reuben had been quite a persuasive fellow, convincing a taxi driver to give him a free ride to the bus depot, and then somehow – heaven knows how – also persuading someone at the bus depot to purchase a ticket for him into Vancouver. When he'd arrived at the depot in Vancouver, he'd simply boarded bus after bus, riding about town, until he'd seen some terrain that was familiar to him. Once he was on familiar ground, the rest was simple.

We listened to this story with some amazement. As the exhausted but relieved searchers left the office, our nurse turned to me, and with a roguish gleam of triumph in her eye, said "Just like a salmon going home!"

It was an encouraging story to all of us. Despite all logic, despite his growing confusion and bewilderment, Reuben knew where he was headed. The way home is marked within us deeper than we know.

Tip of the iceberg

I was once leading a creative writing workshop for a small number of Hallmark elders. My particular slant as facilitator was consistent with my own interests; I'd always been interested in psychology – the reasons *behind* things. When I write, it is often to plumb the vagaries of human nature; our behaviours are icebergs, I think – there is so much beneath the surface, and things are rarely as they seem.

Slightly awed by this group of women gathered around a common desire to write their life stories, none (other than myself) under 80 years old, I nonetheless ventured this approach, looking forward to the depth of insight that their many years might offer. I suggested that they first write about someone in their childhood whom they'd disliked, seeking to answer the question,

"How did she, or he, get to be that way?" While some returned the following week somewhat uncomfortable with the whole idea (after all, it wasn't very *Christian* to dislike anyone), Edna offered a story of injustice written with passion and conviction.

Edna was 88 years old - a powerful woman who'd raised seven children, whose unflinching pragmatism and unfaded wit illustrated how she had survived such a feat. She proceeded to read to us all the story of a young boy who'd sat behind her in grade school. He'd continually terrorized her by pulling her braids and generally tormenting her in any way he could. She then described the day when he'd actually managed to unbutton the top few buttons of her blouse (in those days, buttons were in the back), revealing to all of her classmates in the rows behind her the old and torn camisole she was wearing underneath. This experience thoroughly humiliated her - so much so that, even now, some eighty years later, the voice that read the carefully worded description of the event shook with rage. I knew Edna as a wise and thoughtful woman. Thus, when I asked her, "What do you think made him that way?" I prepared myself for numerous insightful speculations. Edna drew herself up straight and glowered at me over her glasses. "Original sin!" she retorted.

The room fell silent.   An iceberg rolled over sideways, enormous as a whale, and slowly disappeared from sight.

An unfinished conversation

*R*on is someone with whom I carry an unfinished conversation. The last time I saw him, I felt there was something wanting to be said that was not said. And what do you say to someone who is looking out at you from inside a soon-to-depart ambulance, when your eyes meet and you both know that you won't see each other again, at least not on this earth? I felt I was in the presence of a wise, weary and valiant soldier who wanted to hand over his dog tag, and give more than his name, rank and serial number before he left for his final battle. Was there something I could have said to draw out what he wanted to say?

The last talk I'd had with Ron took place some time before. I'd been walking alongside him, listening to him speak of a recent hospital stint, followed by his analysis of the medical care he'd received. This precise recitation of events was, as always, given in his clipped Australian accent, and, even though he now had a slight stoop and an aged shuffle, his regal air prevailed. I'd thought incredulously, "I am walking down the hall with a former Supreme Court judge, and he is telling me about his bowel obstruction." Nonetheless, experiences of the body equalize us all, and the poultice of telling is needed for such traumas. So I listened, and felt honoured at the unspoken trust that this conversation offered.

Memory escorts me next into his suite, immaculate and simple, sporting a few pictures of him during the war, a dashing young pilot, all lean energy and angled cheekbones shadowing down to a square firm jaw. Certificates of achievement were hung on the wall too, all of them in a quiet embossed vellum row. There were books everywhere - the only unruly aspect of the room – stacks of them, behind antique glassed-in bookcases, on ornate imported end tables, beside a quietly expensive pair of loveseats. The books were mostly classics, of course – Plato, Socrates, Shakespeare. "And here are the classics of my old age," Ron had said dryly, gesturing toward a pile of British spy novels stacked on the floor beside a mechanical chair that hummed and tipped and rose up so that he didn't have to.

It was beside these novels, on those loveseats, that a colleague and I had sat, soon after he'd moved into Hallmark, listening to Ron's stories; he was an R.A.F. fighter pilot in WWII. It may have been that we were writing a story for a Remembrance Day reading; I no longer remember. I do, however, recall him holding us spell-bound with stories of near-misses both as a pilot-in-training, as well as in the service, stories told as one would expect Ron to tell them - elegantly, and without embellishment. He'd observed that what people said was true – there is something uncommonly precious about the relationships between men fighting in war. His experience of this had been rich and deep and rare – so much so that, to this day, some sixty-five years later, he still missed it keenly. "We were willing to die for each other," he said, "and we trusted each other with our lives." He elaborated on one particularly vivid experience he'd had at the age of 21, flying with joint coalition forces out of Australia on bombing raids in the Micronesia Islands. He'd been squadron leader, and his wingman had been Canadian; they had just finished their raid, exchanged glances, and given each other the thumbs-up, when the wingman and his plane just vaporized, in an explosion so great that Ron's plane had rolled sideways. "One moment, I could see him," said

Ron, choosing his words carefully, "and the next moment he was gone." We sat in shocked silence. "How did you cope with that?" we asked. "That's how it was," said Ron. "Seven men would be at the pre-flight meal, and you knew that by the end of the flight, two or three men would be missing. It was standard protocol."

He looked out the window and away from us; the afternoon sun exposed a thin stream of water sliding down one cheek. It was not comfortable for Ron to show such emotion; respect demanded that we look away. "I am sorry," he said. My gaze went to the photo of the dapper young soldier confidently leaning against a Spitfire, and then returned to the slight form of this elderly man, now more sinew than muscle, more frail than robust. After the war, life went on to bring Ron more battles. One of them was uncommonly heartbreaking. It involved the death of his beloved wife in a tragic accident; Ron had been the driver. Every once in a while, he would speak of this, in impromptu and surprisingly vulnerable conversations offered to me or other staff. His courage won our hearts. He'd been a soldier more than once; his life after the war had asked him to be that valiant again.

Ron's eligible status as a widower did not escape the notice of the female members of our community. Yes, when Ron first walked into our building, more than one pulse began to flutter! Numerous women saw through the façade of physical age to the soldier who walked within.   And, though he was not averse to playing the field just a bit, he did settle into giving his full attention to one woman at a time.   "It's all there," confided Ron's new woman friend with delight to one of our staff, "the sparks, the whole thing. I had no idea this could still happen at my age!"

As senior manager, I too received his full attention at times, though not always the sort of attention one would choose to pursue. His high-ranking career had come with lifestyle expectations which were quite different than most, especially in the realm of cuisine. Ron pointedly brought some of his own food items to the dining room when he felt our versions substandard. Still, there is more to all of us than our preferences; in the end, it was a privilege to walk even the rocky human side of community life with him.

I remember one Christmas Gala – we had live bands and dances - when Ron walked carefully across the floor and asked me to dance. While his mobility was waning, I knew he was still much more adept in the dance department than I. And so I took to the floor with him, apologizing all the way. I was a Mennonite from the prairies, and dance instruction had not been my experience. Despite his initial doubt at my claims of ineptitude, I sensed that he quickly became rather astonished by how many left feet I could actually carry across the dance floor with me. His initial reassurance of, "Don't worry, you're doing just fine," – soon subsided to gallant silence, and he led me around the floor as I continued to trip, lurch sideways, laugh and apologize. He was a true gentleman.

There are other memories, other conversations. But, in the end, that is not what this story is about. Ron, maybe you know why I'm writing this. Perhaps I am trying to find what it is I wanted to say to you – past generational propriety, as one soul to another. While the open emotionality of my generation is a luxury that soldiers of your generation and experience could not afford, still, was there something you'd wanted from me, even needed, even then?

At this point, I find myself in that same place – having just heard you'd been loaded up into an ambulance, and coming outside asking if I could see you. So the driver opened one door, and I leaned in and our eyes met, and I can't for the life of me remember what I said. Regardless, there was a whole other conversation going on between us, unspoken. We both saw the angel death and acknowledged it with our eyes.

And so, all of our former conversations faded before the strength of the one begun at the back door of that ambulance, where I stood as in an old war movie, with my feet on the ground and you propped up on the gurney, looking back out at me as though I were the war nurse, or the beloved one to be left behind as you went off to battle, your final solo foray into the unknown.

Perhaps, if I had at least taken your hand —

Walking with Sarah

*I*n the midst of a rather intense meeting one
morning, I saw a scene that stopped me in my
tracks. A narrow silver cylinder edged into view from
the doorway, soon revealing itself to be the leg of a
walker – Sarah's walker, to be exact. Emerging then -
slowly, slowly - was the figure of eighty-year old Sarah,
painstakingly making her way down the hallway, lifting
one foot up in the air, advancing it a few inches, then
placing it down, transferring her weight then to the other
foot, and so on. And so on. I could not breathe – it was
the world in slow motion: Sarah walking home. It was a
holy moment somehow, and I could not say why. But
that scene replayed often in my head over the next days
and weeks. It haunted me. It companioned me.

A month or so later, I was headed down that same hallway and saw Sarah once more moving towards me - same pace, but different shoes this time. Or should I say shoe? Her one foot was bound in a sock. "I have bunions," she said to me dryly, "and one of them exploded." Now it was even more difficult for Sarah to walk.

As we talked, I was struck by a kind of light around her head and face. No, it did not come from around her; it seemed to come from within her, and it shone through her eyes and her smile. "Sarah," I said, feeling rather foolish, "did you know that you have a glow about you?" Sarah smiled, and glowed even brighter. "I've heard people say that," she said. Then she looked up at me from her bent position over the walker, and said "Thank you for your kindness. These days it's good to know I'm good at something." "Surely you are, Sarah," I replied, "None of us are good at everything, but we all have something to give...at least that's what I'm hoping."

Sarah looked past me down the hall, her brow knitted in thought. Then her face cleared, and she said, "Yes, if we were good at everything, we'd be incomplete."

Smiling, unaware that she'd just dropped a nuclear bomb of wisdom upon me, Sarah carried on into the elevator. And me - I just kept walking.

A century set in gold

Christina toured our retirement residence at the age of 95. "It's very lovely in here, dear," she had said, gently but firmly. "And when I'm *old*, this is where I would like to live." She continued to live independently in her own home and, at the age of 98, she moved into the Hallmark community.

Two years later, I found myself standing outside the door of Christina's suite, armed with a pad and paper, tasked with the rather daunting goal of summarizing her century of living into a one-page article for a local newspaper.

As I perched hopefully across from Christina on her antique couch, she was more interested in discussing my life than hers, but finally we began to work our way through the list of questions I'd made. Then, there was a knock at the door – an old friend dropping in. "Can you return later, please?" Christina asked her, and then, to me, "Sorry dear, where were we?" I opened my mouth - the phone rang, once, and then again. When her second batch of visitors arrived, she suggested I return later on in the week. It was far from the quiet life one might expect of someone soon to reach the century mark.

So far, I had learned she was born in Manitoba in 1903 and was the eldest of ten children ("I know how to take care of children, let me tell you!"). She'd studied Home Economics in a Winnipeg college. Her summer job as a waitress in Glacier National Park brought her into contact with a young theology student hired for the summer to clear excess pebbles from local streams. "We were meant for each other," Christina said simply. "And, as is often the case with women, instead of using my education, I got married."

Christina and George began their life together in Peace River country; he served as an Anglican Rector there, pioneering new churches. Next, they moved to the United States, where he became Canon of one of the largest Episcopalian churches in California. "My husband had great faith," said Christina, "and we always worked together." When they were in their early forties, they moved to Abbotsford to assist his ailing stepmother, and spent their next 42 years there. George continued in parish work for the Anglican Church, and they raised chinchillas; life was full, and busy. When George fell ill, Christina nursed him until his death in 1993. She lived alone in their home until she moved to Hallmark.

I returned to Christina's suite later that week to complete the interview. Sitting across from her once again, I was hoping for a nugget of wisdom, something around which to form her particular story. I'd sensed a deep contentment within her, and wondered what had brought her to that place. To me, she was a woman of dignity, almost queen-like, and also a woman of few words. I wondered if somehow I could write Christina's story as more than a procession of events – where she was born, and where she'd lived – I wondered if I would be able to discern and convey Christina's spirit, despite her reticence. Finally I asked, "If you were sitting across from a group of high school graduates today, what would you say to them?"

Christina fell silent. "Well," she said finally. "Your faith in God is very important." She spoke of the move she and her husband had made from California to Abbotsford. "That decision was hard for me to accept - it was painful to leave our many friends. But my husband had promised his stepmother that when she needed him, he would be there," she said.

She turned then to look out the window. The afternoon light caught the edge of her glasses, her snow-white hair. For a moment, everything was quiet. Then, she turned back to me and said, "Your whole life is an acceptance, really."

That sentence flared into my awareness as the sun might on a gold ring, with one momentary blaze of light. I caught my breath; my pen stilled. I had just been given a gift, a wisdom gleaned from many years of living. I did not need to write that sentence down; I knew it would stay vivid in my memory.

Christina invited me to her kitchen table, and showed me letters and certificates from the Queen, Canada's Prime Minister, the Governor General, BC's Premier – all beautifully embossed on white paper, all honouring her on her 100th birthday. She then pulled out a worn leather-bound address book, held together by two elastic bands, and asked me to write my name inside. There were many names in this book – some of which I recognized – and I wrote my own name carefully on the fragile yellowed paper. To have one's name included in Christina's address book seemed its own rare honour.

As I remember her serene face that day, I wonder what Christina was like as a young girl, a young woman, a middle-aged woman. I wonder about the struggles and difficulties that were weathered in order for her to arrive at that one elegant statement, and seemingly to be at rest there. Those life struggles will not be spoken - not by Christina; they have been lived, and are gone. What remains, from a century of living, is an acceptance of things – a pearl of great price. Hold it up to the light, ponder it - put it in a setting of gold. One person earned it, hard, with her body and her blood. And gives it to you when her story is done.

Things that matter

Self-consciousness has been my middle name. Well, actually, my parents awarded me the middle name of 'Rose', but I've been self-conscious about that too, considering roses to be the stuff of overly sentimental poetry. As I get older though, and begin to unabashedly fall in love with the beauty – and yes, the sweet scent – of roses, I thank my parents for my middle name. When I was younger, I didn't want to be seen as sentimental; I wanted to be detached, and unaffected.

But on to the story I want to tell. One afternoon, I went to visit one of our residents in the hospital. She had had a tough go of it for a very long time and lay there in her bed, quite discouraged. When I arrived, I didn't know what to say to her. Any words I could think of seemed trite in the face of her suffering, and I did not want to belittle or diminish what she was going through in any way. I knew she was of faith, and I knew her generation had an abundance of hymns with which they would have grown up; it would have been their mother's milk. Thankfully, it was mine as well; I still love hymns, more and more as I get older. So, in the absence of any words of my own, I asked her if she would like to sing a hymn with me. She said "yes" instantly, so we came up with one we both knew and began to sing. I remember my voice squeaking on the high notes. I remember losing track of which words went where. I remember one verse where she and I both trailed off at the same point, and looked at each other, clearly hoping the other one had the words, but neither of us did. She was physically frail, and her voice petered out pretty quickly; so I was often left singing – if you could call it that - on my own, feeling quite self-conscious. Still, she joined in here and there as she could, and we warbled our way to the finish. I don't remember what else ensued in that visit; I don't remember our conversation. I just remember us singing together, and a sense of solace at the end. And then, I carried on.

I moved on to another ward to visit an aunt of mine – a dear, wise and beautiful aunt who was in her nineties. With me, I carried a sweet memory of visiting her apartment when she still lived independently with her aging husband. Aunt Susan had put together a full lunch for the three of us, and had seated herself across from me at the table. I remember the dishes - a familiar old china pattern, the small bowl of creamy potato salad, fried chicken pieces piled in a bowl, alongside some farmer sausage. The dill pickles were chilled and sliced thin, just the way I liked them. She had baked cinnamon buns from scratch, and they looked delicious. I remember how, after she'd said grace for the meal, she'd looked up from her folded hands and said, "I was reading the other day that people spend too much time talking about each other, and not enough time talking about what matters - ideas, or important events happening in the world." She'd looked at me with a gentle smile, and asked, "So…what do you think about our prime minister?" From there, we'd carried on a lively conversation that went from politics to history to theology – the things that mattered to us. I wasn't sure which had been sweeter – the pure spirit of Aunt Susan or her cinnamon buns. And yes, maybe I digress into undignified sentiment, but…maybe I don't. It matters. For whatever reason, it matters.

So here I was, years later, visiting Aunt Susan in the hospital, where she was recovering from a hip replacement. We chatted for awhile, and I said, "Aunt Susan, you know, I've always been self-conscious about my voice. And you know too, how Mom has such a great voice – well, mine isn't so great. The beautiful voice I hear in my head sounds a lot different than the one that comes out of my mouth. Anyway, I just went to visit one of our residents in the hospital, and she wanted me to sing a hymn with her, so I did. And I couldn't remember the words, Aunt Susan; I couldn't carry the tune all that well either, and there were other people in the room, so I felt quite foolish." Aunt Susan shifted slightly in her bed, her eyes not leaving my face.

"Finally," I said, "I just decided to leave my ego at the door and do what had to be done."

"Good for you," she replied with a smile, her eyes sharp with understanding, "Now you can be *useful!*"

Collections and connections

eacups and saucers. China dolls, Christmas cards, porcelain figurines and train sets. Collections of things - old letters and greeting cards, piled and falling out of closet shelves and dresser drawers - the things we cannot throw away. When you've moved from a large house to the compact space of retirement, what you choose to keep says a lot about what matters to you. It says a lot about your life.

Norm had his train set. It was a joy and a trial, that set. It was clearly too big for his suite, and indeed too precious for him to give up. We cleared a space in a small third floor storage room; he would only need a bit of room, he thought, and just for a few months until he could make other storage arrangements. Two years later, the train still whistled happily on command, along a lovely oblong track that took up most of that room. For a time, the set was relocated to the underground scooter garage, and then returned to the third floor once again, to what seemed to be its permanent home. Many a time, a staff member, in dire need of storage space, would say resolutely, "I'm going to talk to Norm," but would return, cowed and strangely silent. Who could ask Norm to part with his train set? It seemed an unfeeling, inhuman request.

Housekeeping staff saw the collections inside each resident's suite, and, every week, cleaned around them: family pictures crowding walls and shelves, stacks of books, photos of antique cars, war medals and uniforms. Some were less visible than others; some were collections of wrongdoings, of unfair behaviours, of unjust treatment, or events. Others were collections of blessings, built on an inherent belief in goodness. For the most part, we all learned to move relatively smoothly around the many collections that existed within our small community.

One morning, we held a "doll show" in the Square inside our front entrance. Two residents were avid doll-collectors – Edie had at least forty of them in her suite. The dolls were out on display that morning – bride dolls, nurse dolls, baby dolls, dolls in ethnic dress - every imaginable kind of doll. For one brief hour – from eleven till twelve - folks came by and took a look while Edie and Casey sat proudly alongside their "charges".

At about five minutes past noon, I was walking down the hall. Everyone was in the dining room, not a soul around, except Edie. There she sat beside her doll collection with an empty cup of coffee, looking at something I could not see. "Skipping lunch today, Edie?" asked our Concierge cheerfully a few minutes later as she returned to the front office. "Yes," answered Edie, without moving. A while later, I saw Edie heading down the hall in her scooter. She returned with two more dolls in her basket. "Adding more?" I asked inanely, sensing her need for the display to continue on, her need for this collection to have an audience.

There was an emptiness in the square as I asked this, that loneliness that people feel when something long-anticipated is over – a special event, a wedding - and you are left only with yourself, and something to clean up. It was a loneliness that followed me into my office, and I sat with the door ajar, with that ache for Edie, for myself, for something that can't be possessed, but only given. It can only come to us as gift.

And then Mary came into the square: "I've come to look at all these dolls. Which ones are yours, Edie? Hey, I have a Santa doll just like that!", and, "Which one's your favourite?"

Speedy Edie

One of our stated community values at Hallmark is 'the freedom to risk'. Not typical, maybe, for your average retirement community, but there it is. You couldn't have an owner like Stan Hindmarsh without having a bit of an edge to things. Stan is a freedom fighter who believes that the worst thing that can happen is not failure or injury, but to not try at all. With Stan in the lead, we work to integrate that belief into the day-to-day. It adds spice to things, for sure. One year, preparations were well under way for the second annual Scooter Race, to be held in our L-shaped parking lot. The buzz had started weeks before. Competition knows no age, and this was certainly evidenced in the good-natured taunting taking place in the halls. Residents sported brightly-coloured hats and racing attire, and took their scooters out for sidewalk "spins" that were much faster than usual.

The morning of the Scooter Race dawned, clear and sunny, and the event was ready to go – complete with checkered flags, markers, and volunteers with stopwatches and clipboards. Friends, family, and staff turned up to cheer.

Competitors emerged from the front door of the building. All had made an effort to express their individuality in costumes for the occasion; "Stormin' Norman" showed up in train engineer overalls and a polka dotted scarf. And out the side door, attired in red, came "Speedy Edie". She'd earned that title righteously, her granddaughter Karena told us, as she'd always had a lead foot.

Ninety year-old Edie had entered the race the previous year, but then she had "only" placed. The "only" was Edie's disclaimer. The rest of us considered the fact that she was legally blind, and thus felt that her participation alone was an exceptional feat. However, she informed us all that this year, she was determined to win. To her, the fact that she couldn't see was clearly a minor detail beside the strength of her ambition. The rest of us were a bit nervous about Edie entering the race, but, it was her choice – we believed in the "freedom to risk", right?

The race began. One by one, elders carefully – or recklessly – guided their scooters around the markers, then sped, to raucous cheering and whoops, down the final stretch and across the finish line. Stormin' Norman, ball cap on backwards, completed the course in good time, setting a high standard, which was well-matched by the next competitor. Then it was Edie's turn. The flag went down, and so did her lead foot. "Slow down, Edie!" hollered someone in the crowd, and others took up the call. Edie hunched down over the handlebars, and pressed her foot down harder. With her red sweater flying and fire in her eyes, Edie cruised handily around the first markers. Her time so far was great! But next thing you know, she took a sharp corner too fast. Her scooter tipped, and there was Edie, lying on the ground. It was at this point that we learned that "Speedy Edie" had upped her scooter speed, from the recommended "turtle" setting to "rabbit". People ran to her aid from every direction. It appeared that Edie had hurt her arm. We wanted to call an ambulance, but she wouldn't hear of it. While her son Steve drove her to the hospital, he'd asked, "Mom, why full throttle?" Edie had replied, "Well, it's a *race* isn't it?"

By this time, I was not the only staff member actively questioning our "freedom to risk" policy. There were tears and questions, and a soberness settled over the event. Should we continue with the event? Should we shut it down? Finally, Steve called from the hospital to inform us that Edie had a scraped arm, a sprained wrist, and a few bruises, but was otherwise fine. "Well, she's not exactly fine," he said, hesitating; "she's really mad." My heart stopped. I held my breath, waiting for the well-deserved rebuke that surely would follow. Steve continued: "Mom's mad that she fell. All the way to the hospital she kept saying, 'I want to finish that race!' She wants me to ask you '*when's the next one?*'"

Marnie remembered

I 'm remembering Marnie today, how she showed me through her family albums, old pictures of her mother, her siblings. "They're all gone now," she said, and turned another page. Even the photographs were fading. I felt us both turn sepia in the room even while I marvelled at her sister's beauty, the wistful melancholy in her mother's eyes. Marnie was to be 87 soon; she believed she would then fade away, that after her this birthday, she would either die, or Jesus would come again. "Would that Jesus would come now," I said to her, grinning and lifting myself out of the chair; "I wouldn't have to do any more paperwork."

Early in Hallmark's existence, when everything was new and all of us were working long hours, I went down to the kitchen, well into the supper hour to see if I could fill up a plate. Glancing into the dining room to see who was still there, I headed over to the table where Marnie and her husband were sitting. It was already late, and soon her husband stood up to leave. Marnie asked me, "Do you mind if we go and leave you alone?" "No problem at all," I said, "I like being with people, and I also like being alone." Marnie nodded; "I like my own company as well." But then she moved to sit down with me. "You don't have to stay," I protested; "honestly, I'm just fine." "Oh, no," she said, "I think this is a fortuitous moment." She proceeded to tell me that she'd been a secretary for many years, but didn't like it, "because people too often called when I was enjoying my own company." She grinned. "I *like* you, Marnie," I said.

She'd been raised in a family of six siblings. Her mother had died when she was quite young, as had a brother. "There was much sorrow in our home," she said. Her hands were laced with blue veins, one shaking slightly on the table, the other encircling her water glass. "But we were still glad to be together as we were." She paused for a moment, looking at me, as though approaching a fork in a road and deciding which way to turn, maybe what direction to take the conversation. "All my siblings are dead," she said. "That must feel strange," I replied. "Yes," she said quickly, her eyes burning into mine, pushing aside barriers and safe places. "I feel very odd. I have no one to ask about my life or childhood anymore. It used to be that when I couldn't remember something that happened way back, I could just pick up the phone, and call one of my siblings. My older sister had the best memory. Now there is no one to call, and I am forgetting more every day. Some days, it feels like I am actually disappearing. Maybe one day, I'll be invisible."

Then Marnie had to go. I asked if I could give her a hug. "I rather thrive on hugs," she said, and we held on to each other for a moment, with tenderness. She said, "I love you, Melody," and as we pulled away from each other, I felt taken aback, awash in this miracle, gasping for air like a fish while she, having dispensed all this love, calmly looked at her watch and said, "We must go now; tomorrow is another day."

This, my first conversation with Marnie, was recorded in my journal entry made nearly a decade ago. The friendship that we shared for the next few years was a fond one, and full of tender moments. And, while details often slide, wily and formless as sand, through the fingers of my memory, thankfully, I did write some of them down. Like the time I attended the community birthday party, for instance. There was a huge rectangular cake festooned with a thick layer of whipping cream, magnificent, and glistening like snow. Marnie and I approached it with a mixture of reverence and greed. "When I was a child," she said, "I always wanted to stick my finger into the icing." "Marnie, you're almost 90," I responded, "When exactly do you think the time will be right?" She laughed and purposefully swiped her finger through a good length of whipped cream, licking it off with great satisfaction.

Then there was the time when a housekeeper was sick, and a few of us stepped in to help clean. For the next week, every time I met Marnie in the hallway, she'd crow, "When I go to sleep, I think, '*Melody* made this bed!'" One small gesture met with great reward; I basked in Marnie's extravagant love. In Marnie's suite, I was always met with welcome, our conversations characterized by honesty, humour, and a mutual appreciation for a clever turn of phrase.

Marnie's health waned over the years, and there came the day that I visited her in the hospital emergency ward. I bent over, not to hug her – her body felt too fragile and I was afraid of hurting her - but just to put my cheek against hers. "My Melody," she said then, patting the back of my head gently, "my Melody." Even then, Marnie's love - familiar, but never common – was generously offered.

Marnie has indeed now passed on to 'the other side', as she in her later years often wished to do. Sometimes, it feels like the details of our friendship are disappearing too, fading like old photographs, dust-covered and kept in a box somewhere. And someday my own life will disappear, and then, forgotten, that box of photos will go out with the trash.

I can't help but feel that Marnie's eyes still burn with life somewhere, that in the end, everything that matters is remembered, stored somewhere in a Greater Memory.

In the meantime, there is this earth. Marnie had a picture of the Wailing Wall in Jerusalem over her bed. It was significant to her, and she once told me why. However, sadly, that memory has faded, and I have no one to call to get it back.

Tim in the sun

/ 've known you for over six years now!" I said
to the elderly man curled up on the bed across
from where I was sitting. Tim, now 79 years old, smiled,
gulped and dropped his head as emotion washed over
his face. He'd been this way since his first stroke –
emotional. "Yup," he said. "Many years." My gaze
strayed over to the chest of drawers in the corner of the
room, upon which sat the small red wool snowman I'd
given him for Christmas a number of years before. I'd
given it to him on a whim – or, perhaps, on a 'nudge';
but for him clearly it was no whim. It was one of the
few things he had displayed on his dresser. Beside it sat
a photo of his father, his mother, and a niece's wedding.
"Still have that snowman, huh, Tim?" I asked. "Yup,"
he said.

When Tim had moved into Hallmark, I'd felt an instant though inexplicable connection with him. We had little in common. In one early conversation, I'd asked him what he'd enjoyed most about his job as assistant librarian in a remote prairie school. He'd looked around him, as if to ensure no one else would hear, dropped his voice, and whispered, "I love the Dewey Decimal System." That should have been enough to end the conversation, but strangely, it was the beginning of something more.

His life was a fascinating and often sad story, the details of which emerged over time. Our nurse, who had visited him in his home before he moved into our residence, noted him as fearful and very reluctant to leave the confines of his small apartment. When he moved in to Hallmark soon after, his ducked head and shuffling gait became a familiar part of our community, and always a beloved sight to me.

"Do you know why I moved in?" he asked me one day, while we were having coffee and a cookie one afternoon. "The whole time the lady was showing me around, I kept thinking 'I don't belong here.' But then, when I was leaving, she gave me a hug. I thought, 'maybe I could live here after all'."

Most people steered clear of Tim. He had an irritating habit of correcting people's grammar, as well as their behaviour. Still, he took to hugs – for we were a huggy bunch of staff – and held on to the hugger as if he were drowning. This became more and more the case over time, until hugging Tim became something for which I had to prepare myself emotionally, since whenever I sought to extricate myself, it felt as if I were tearing something in two.

One time I was facilitating a creative writing workshop with a small group of elders. For the first assignment, I asked everyone to think about someone they disliked in their younger years – and then to write a story about how that person became that way. Surprisingly, Tim showed up at the second workshop and sat, fidgeting, while a few people read their stories. When I asked him if he had anything to share, he spoke at length about how he couldn't write anymore because of his stroke, and how he wasn't a writer anyway. Then he said "But I'd still like to talk about my teacher." He then told us about his first elementary school teacher, who - convinced that Tim was slow and stupid - would stand in frustration at arm's length from the boy, stiffen his own arms, and slap Tim on one side of the head and the other until he was too tired to continue. There was a silence in the room as Tim spoke. He continued doggedly, despite sympathetic noises from those of us listening in horror. "I've been thinking about why he might have behaved that way, and I think now that maybe his own school experience was even worse than mine. Maybe he was being kinder to me than his own teachers had been to him, and he was just doing the best he could." We sat silent for a time. Then the next person began to read her story.

Later in the hallway, I found Tim, and asked him if he was going to come back to the next meeting. He swept my question aside and asked, "Do you know why I told that story?" My mind went blank; I was still unsettled by his description of his teacher. "Because I needed to be free of it," he said. As he shuffled off down the hall, he turned back and added: "Next time I'm going to talk about my dog. It's a much better story."

I saw Tim most often in the library, a place he seemed to frequent almost daily. Straightening books, aligning them by subject and height, was a familiar pastime to him. One time, I poked my head in the door, and said, "Hey Tim! I'm having a bad day. Do you know a joke or something?" He responded, not with a joke, but with a poem he had memorized:

Leisure

by William Henry Davies

What is this life if, full of care,
We have no time to stand and stare.
No time to stand beneath the boughs
And stare as long as sheep or cows.
No time to see, when woods we pass,
Where squirrels hide their nuts in grass.

No time to see, in broad daylight,
Streams full of stars like skies at night.
No time to turn at Beauty's glance,
And watch her feet, how they can dance.
No time to wait till her mouth can
Enrich that smile her eyes began.
A poor life this, if, full of care,
We have no time to stand and stare.

Those words were just what my sore heart needed to hear. The contemplative side of me had always had a deep desire to do just this, to have time to 'stand and stare' - yet my work often placed me in roles where there was much to be done, and often at a fast pace. Unknowingly, Tim had painted a picture of my longing for tranquility and solitude. Not long after, I returned to Tim and asked him to recite the poem for me again. He looked bewildered and couldn't remember which poem I meant. "It's about sitting and waiting, I think," I said. He looked embarrassed, then mischievous. "I can't tell you that one!" he said. "Oh, come on, Tim, why not?" I asked. He lowered his eyes and said the only poem about sitting and waiting that he could remember was a boyhood one involving a bathroom. We had a good laugh.

My role at Hallmark changed; I moved into the corporate office, and was not as involved in the daily workings of the community. I saw Tim less frequently; time was short, it seemed – there was even less time to 'stand and stare'. The odd time I'd see him in the dining room, and would go over and talk with him, briefly. By then he was retreating more and more into himself; he'd had several strokes. He made it very clear though, every time he saw me, that he cared very much about me. What had I done to deserve this kindness, this regard, I thought guiltily; I hardly saw him any more. Yet, there it was, Tim's love, for free.

A few years later, I returned from a long holiday to find, in my overstuffed inbox, a small handwritten note from the concierge. "Tim would like to see you, Melody, when you have time." That afternoon, I sat down in his suite, on a worn plaid chair that smelled faintly of mould. I looked at him, curled up on the bed like an old leaf. "What are you up to these days, Tim?" I asked.

"Not very much," he said.

"Do you get outside and walk?" I asked.

"Not really." he said.

We exchanged a few more sentences, and I took the plunge. "You said you wanted to talk with me." I braced myself, expecting criticism of something Hallmark had or hadn't done. "Was there something in particular you'd wanted to talk about?"

He looked confused. "I just wanted to see you," he said, "I don't get to see you very often."

Head down, he asked if, sometime, I might want to go for a walk with him. I glanced at my watch; I had about half an hour. "How about now? Just a short walk to the park, to the edge of the water? It's not far at all." So he and I shuffled down the hall to the door.

It was a sunny spring afternoon. I inhaled deeply, gratefully filling my lungs with the sweet fresh air. Tim moved his feet a few inches at a time. I had to slow my step to match his, and whenever I asked a question, he would stop to answer. At this rate, I thought, sneaking a glance at the rapidly advancing hands of my watch, we'd reach the park by nightfall. Just then, Tim stopped once more. "Look at that," he said, pointing at a cherry tree in full bloom, lacy pink. "Look at those flowers," he added, gesturing towards a clutter of dark purple pansies.

The walk was long for Tim, yet short in time. When we returned to his suite, I gave him a hug; he returned it, as he had for years, with an intense life-gulping clutch, his forehead hot against my turned cheek. When I released him, he reached out and touched my face, deliberately and gently with his hand. And then I returned to my office, and he to his suite.

Why am I writing about Tim? Why is his story so close to me? I wondered this as something so deep within so as to be inarticulate, pushed the words of Tim's story out from my memory, through my heart, and onto this page. And then I knew. In some way, Tim is

me, he is my life unlived. Tim is my desire to hide from
life, to withdraw to a safe place where no one can find
me. And this part of me, like Tim, is constantly in need
of love, of fresh air, of getting out of that room in which
she hides. Not for any great purpose, except this: to be
alive together. And so we walk together, faltering, and
slow, down the path to the water. "One time," he'd said
to me that afternoon, with conviction in his voice, "we'll
walk over to that bench over there by the river, and
that's where we'll be for a very long time."

Practically artistic

*D*on and I are about as different as they come. He is an inherently practical man, drawn to the world of matter and materials; I am a writer and visual artist, given to flights of imagination and conceptual thought. Don spends hours each day operating woodworking machines – a band saw, a lathe, belt sanders. He measures length and width, engineering things so that they fit together precisely and function like clockwork. He produces mantel clocks, wooden trucks with winches, and piles of blocks in their boxes. He turns out children's toys with pieces that follow carefully angled tracks, yo-yos that spin in the air, colourful tops that whirl concentric circles across any surface. He inlays coloured wood laminate into precise rose patterns on wooden jewellery boxes.

I'll admit, it's difficult for me to navigate the 'physical' world at times. I'm easily distracted from it - often deep in conversation about the meaning of life, ferreting out the essence of some complex behaviour, or just simply cloud-watching. I've had to get used to being seen as absent-minded, and often having the 'conceptual' world – *my* world – dismissed as irrelevant. While it stings sometimes, it is indeed pretty funny how, for example, I can drive down the road while quite oblivious to the road itself.

When I visited Don in his workshop, therefore, I dutifully laid my 'artistic' self aside; I thought that was what he wanted – what everyone wanted – and did my best to follow the logical conversation, the well-engineered layout of his mind, and its resultant good works. Our conversations typically consisted of detailed descriptions of how a certain toy was made, and with which kind of wood. I came to see him as yet another example of why his kind of personality and approach were better for the world. I had only to recall him on the floor in a Guatemalan orphanage, surrounded by chattering children, demonstrating how one toy or another worked, to know that a mind focused on tangibles brought tangible gifts to the world. Things people needed. Things people could see.

Don had taken up carpentry as a hobby after his retirement from 39 years at BC Hydro. He was in his late 80's when he moved into Hallmark; I remember the weeks that preceded that decision. He'd told our marketer in no uncertain terms that if there was no place to do woodwork, he wouldn't move in. "I wanted to keep my hands in something productive," he told me later. "What it all would lead to, I had no idea."

What it led him to, and through, was a deeper journey into the "joy of giving". Those words seem simple, and are spoken easily. But those relatively unremarkable three words do not sufficiently encompass what had been birthed through their practise in that workshop, day after day, piece by piece, in block after block of wood. It took me a long time to see what Don was doing. I was distracted by the small practical details that Don lived every day in that workshop, cutting pieces of wood and fitting them together into something to be given away. I had missed the depth of how Don was living; I simply had no idea of the artistry of his work, his life.

I'd visited Don many times in the workshop, popping in for this or that in the context of our annual service trips to Guatemala. Even before he joined those trips, he was willing to contribute, sending along his handcrafted wooden toys for the children. But who was Don Moore? I had no idea. Clearly, he had a generous heart...but those words didn't touch it either. How could I, with my 'artsy' sensibility, often moving in an unseen world, connect with someone so anchored in the physical?

This brings me to my most recent connection with Don. During one of our earlier Guatemala trips, I had seen a brightly-coloured crucifix painted by an indigenous artist. It was the most hopeful cross I'd ever seen, and I too wanted to express that hope – the concept was beautiful. To do so, I needed a cross made of two pieces of flat wood upon which to paint. And so, I made another trip, down the long hall leading to the Hallmark workshop, to talk to Don.

Of course, Don being Don, he was happy to make it. And so he provided the foundation of wood which I needed to paint the concept of hope. The finished cross went up for auction to raise funds for Guatemala, and it sold well. Following the event, a few others asked for a hopeful cross as well, and Don offered to make more wooden 'canvases' for me to paint on. It presented a bit of a dilemma for me; I had painted the first one out of a desire to interact personally with its images, and it was an unexpected pleasure that others connected with it. Charging for this kind of 'sacred' imagery just didn't feel right to me. Especially since, in this case, I was working largely with someone else's images. Still, at the same time, each painting took Don's time to fashion the wooden base, and mine to complete. I went back and forth, pondering numerous options and rationales. Finally, I headed down the hall to the workshop. Don listened to my ideas, but was respectfully reticent with his own thoughts. Finally I asked directly, "Don, what would you do?" He said, "I would give the crosses to them and, if they asked about payment, I would say: 'if you'd like to donate something to the orphans in Guatemala, it's up to you.'" Something deep within me clicked into place. Yes, that was the right approach. "I like it!" I said with relief. "That way how much - if any - is given, is God's problem, not mine."

"God doesn't have a problem." Don replied, with just a shimmer of laughter in his voice. And there you have it – a light went on for me. Don's practical solution had a mystical component. A blending of opposites.

In his actions and now with his words, Don had shared his world with me, opened the door into the wisdom that fed him, body and soul: 'just give, and all that is needed will be given.' To some, Don's formula may seem somewhat...well, impractical. But there is a world beneath it that embraces me, and beckons me to live, as I was created, as I was born – to make tangible the intangible just by living it. By writing it down. By telling this story.

Cyril in love

While recognizing that death is part of the life of any community, we were surprised when one resident's family members requested to use Hallmark as the location for their mother's memorial – and asked the staff to put together the actual service as well. This was a first for us. We were honoured by the request, and did what we could to infuse each aspect of the service with the love we felt for Edith. Members of our staff leadership spoke, prayed, and sang songs requested by the family. Staff got up and shared fond and funny stories about Edith, and finally her grandson gave the eulogy.

All the while, Edith's husband Cyril sat quietly in the front row. I think he knew without question that he was not alone - either in his sorrow or in his life. It was clear that the community embraced him fully. For the tea following the memorial service, Hallmark's cooks used Edith's recipe to make Cyril's favourite dessert: orange chiffon cake.

While the dishes were being cleared away, I went up to Cyril, keenly aware that he and Edith had been together for over sixty years, and had been exceptionally close. He was still sitting in a chair close to her urn of ashes at the front of the room. What could I say? I gave him a hug. "I love you, Cyril," I said. Clear-eyed and at peace, he looked right back into my eyes and said, "I love you too, Melody. Always have."

'*Always have!*' I thought, '*who said that?* Who loves that utterly on the day of their beloved's funeral? Is there no end to love?'

Mary at the elevator

I have followed with interest the story of renowned physicist Stephen Hawking, whose theories on time have provided my busy imagination with much entertainment. I love mystery; I've never had trouble believing in things beyond - anything is possible. Even life beyond time.

'Wouldn't it be great,' I thought, 'if stories written now could somehow also rewrite the past? What if new options could be imagined that curb the influence of a historical event, and alter its trajectory, thus changing the future?'

I was whirling about on this rather entertaining hamster wheel one day when I caught sight of Mary coming down the hall, her hair a small white cloud about her head, thin fingers bent around the black grips of her walker.

Mary and I had met several years back, when she moved into Hallmark after her husband's death. I still remember the day I walked past the Fireside Room and heard the familiar melody of a traditional hymn being played. I stuck my head in the door, and there was Mary, dandelion-gone-to-seed hair around her head, at the piano. She told me that playing hymns was her source of strength and joy. I thanked her for playing them; to hear them consoled me as well. That was the beginning of the bond between Mary and me - a bond of spirit, rooted in our common search for strength, for transcendence of life's challenges.

And so it was that on this day, as always, I was delighted to catch sight of Mary. I'd been rushing down the hall, keys in hand and out of time, already thinking about the next thing I had to do. Thankfully, I did become momentarily aware of my surroundings, aware of her slight frame quietly making its way down the hall and towards the elevator. "Hi Mary!" I said with pleasure. She looked up, said hello, and then, after a moment, added with some energy, "It's *you!*"

"How are you?" she asked, and I told her. I'd just that week completed a reasonable final draft of my first novel. "Thirteen years ago I started it," I said. "It feels great to get this far!"

We spoke about writing for a time, and I asked her if she wrote or journaled. In the past, she'd shared with me about her periodic struggles with depression, a dark burden that weighed upon her. I wondered aloud if writing - which had often helped me with my own darkness - might strengthen her also.

"I used to write," she said, and told me that she'd started to write her memoirs, beginning with her birth. "I wrote up to the time when my parents died; then I didn't write any further." she said, "I was 17 when that happened. I was very green, working as a housekeeper. I had to grow up very fast."

"There is too much there, too much that I don't want to remember," she said. As we stood talking, I realized she was no longer looking at me. It seemed she was looking down into what I imagined was a very old wound, which gaped beneath her like a red nerve-rimmed abyss. I was reminded of what physicists have named the 'event horizon', the place that rims the black hole, where space and time ends, a place initially thought to absorb all light.

"Anyway," she continued, "I don't know what to do with those memoirs – who'd want to read them? Maybe I'll just destroy them." To me, those words sounded more like a question than a statement. Then, "My brother wrote his story. He was a very good writer, but when he died we couldn't find anything. We checked more than once, and there was nothing." "That's a real loss," I said. "Yes," said Mary. "Do you think your children might feel the same loss if you destroyed what you've written?" I asked. "Yes," said Mary, seemingly with reluctance, "I think so."

It was time to go. As I left Mary, I felt sadness at her ongoing struggle. At the same time, I also felt lighter; after all these years of knowing Mary, I now had a clearer insight into that darkness that ebbed and flowed in her being, sure as a tide. It was the untimely loss of her parents - an event-related sadness, frozen in time, and seemingly imprinted on every page she'd turned since that day. A black hole.

Stephen Hawking's initial understanding of black holes was that they destroyed everything that entered them, that no life could survive its force. But Hawking later altered his understanding, saying that information, or life, could re-emerge, although in a form unrecognizable from what went in.[1] So the current suggestion is that there *is* life - in and after - the black hole, albeit in an altered state.

As I pondered this physicist's theories, I was filled with wonder; it felt as though I was looking over his shoulder into the beginnings of the universe. Particles, matter, the passage - even illusion - of time...here, in this powerful mysterious place, was a magnitude of possibility that boggled the mind.

And so, I am given the audacity to hope. That Mary's story could be transformed. That it could still be written as one in which she could flourish, one where the light of the love she has for her parents is not wholly swallowed in the black hole of grief and loss, but rather intensified and transformed into something else - something about survival, even goodness. Where somehow, as inexplicably as the underpinnings of this world can lurch or change, she could re-emerge from that black hole – coughed out, released like a swimmer onto the shore. And that somehow that new story could come to Mary so she could enter and live it – so that, within the mystery of consciousness and existence and the illusion of time, she could try it all again.

A fair bit of time passes before I return to Mary's suite for a visit. Still, as friendship knows no time, we begin at the same depth we always do. We talk about our lives, then about writing. I read her a story, and she listens intently. She then looks with regret at her hands lying in her lap. "They shake a lot," she says. "It is difficult for me to write."

I will do this, I think. I will return as often as I can to Mary's suite, and, if she wants, she can tell me her story. Perhaps, through that telling, we can cheat the conclusions of time and space. Maybe together we can loop back into the past, loop it together with the present and the future, wend together a fabric of hope, and be part of the evolution of this universe that is also resolution. Perhaps not. But we can try.

Road trip with a twist

*R*oad trips, no matter how simple they may seem at the outset, can end up quite different than planned. Here's one with a unique twist…

Two elderly gentlemen once frequented the same table in the Hallmark dining room – Bernard couldn't remember, and Len couldn't see. Bernard had a good heart though, and when he learned that Len's wife Mary had taken ill, he offered to drive him to the hospital that very day to visit her. "Sounds like a good idea," said Len. Even though the MSA Hospital was only about a 10 minute journey from Hallmark, he wasn't able to drive himself because of his limited vision. After supper that day, at about 6:00 pm, they set off.

Shortly after midnight, staff became aware that Len and Bernard had not returned to their suites. They called MSA Hospital. None of the nurses knew if Len and Bernard had been to visit Mary, but they did know that all visitors had left.

A phone call was placed to Bernard's grandson, who hadn't seen them either. The next call went straight to the MSA Hospital emergency department. They confirmed that they had seen neither hide nor hair of the two gentlemen.

At 12:30 a.m., Hallmark notified the police department that Len and Bernard had not come home. While the police traced Bernard's license plate in their registry, staff checked the Hallmark parking lot once more; indeed, the car was not there. By 1:00 a.m., two police officers had arrived at Hallmark's front door to check into the situation further.

At 1:30 a.m., Bernard's car drove into the parking lot, and a very tired Len and Bernard walked in the front door. Len was reported to be "very cross". They had been out driving for seven hours, "lost"; he claimed that they had gone east as far as the town of Hope (about an hour's drive) and also visited the Abbotsford airport - south of town – sometime in between. It was difficult to put the pieces together, as the travellers themselves had not yet accomplished that feat. However, as far as we could tell, at one point they had also visited Chilliwack, a small town about half an hour *east* of Abbotsford.

They'd panicked at the Chilliwack exit, as it was under construction, and cluttered with signs, pylons and flashing markers. Nonetheless, Bernard, ever-determined to deliver his friend to the bedside of his beloved wife, crashed the car through the barricades, and, undeterred, managed to get on the road coming back towards Abbotsford and that ever-elusive MSA Hospital. Somehow though, they then passed the Abbotsford exits and ended up on a rural road in Langley, a Vancouver suburb about 20 minutes *west* of Abbotsford. By this point, they'd been on the road for about six hours. Then, inevitably, Bernard's car ran out of gas. There they were, well into darkness with their car stopped in the middle of an unknown road. They tried to flag down several vehicles. Why in heaven's name *wouldn't* someone stop for two grumpy old men standing beside an older-vintage car in the middle of the night? Finally, some guys in a pickup truck did just that, and took Bernard to a nearby gas station. Bernard was returned to Len and the car shortly thereafter, with a litre or two of gas in a small can (Len said, "Guy's such a cheap Mennonite he only puts $2 worth of gas in his car!"). Thankfully, by this time, they were on the home stretch, although they didn't know it. Shortly afterwards, a police cruiser identified their license plate number, and redirected them to Abbotsford.

The next morning, when Len came down to breakfast, Bernard offered to drive him to the hospital to visit his wife…

Elaine and the golden years

I love being 85 - I've *escaped!*" said Elaine, fluttering her hands beside her head like she was doing the Charleston. In that moment, I didn't think to ask her what it was that she'd escaped. Maybe the perceived tyranny of work, maybe the drudgery of dishes and cooking. Now, in her quiet suite, she had opportunities to linger, for quiet cups of tea, for books piled willy-nilly on her ottoman and table. She had time to contemplate the beautiful paintings she'd collected over the years. Time to notice. Time to *be*.

And I loved to *be* with Elaine. The stairs up to her place travelled light under my feet, her welcome at the door exuberant as a teen.

Elaine's home was filled with small beautiful things, well-loved, and often tied to nature. Birds featured large in her home – drawings of birds, wee ceramic and wooden birds hopping along her window ledges. And then there was her deck - bird-friendly to be sure - with several feeders always topped up. It was a home of poetry, paintings, and of Elaine, ready at a moment's notice to offer a cup of tea, accompanied by something sweet, in her small sitting room that overlooked the park. This was Elaine in her 'digs'. ("This isn't *home* to me," Elaine said one day, gesturing around her. "This is simply a temporary journey into another lifestyle, another time. I don't call it home. I call it 'the digs'.")

I catch myself writing as if she is no longer here, in her bright space by the park. I smile ruefully as I recognize this old pattern of mine – often, when I find myself becoming attached to someone, I imagine them dead, no doubt to protect or prepare myself.

Indeed, somehow it feels safer to write as though she is gone, as though Elaine is a great open field I can see out my window, healed and quiet, with grasses waving in the wind, rather than what she is to me now – a wound and a longing, a longing for a friend like her, someone with whom you simply open your soul, like a seed does in order to flower, and let life in. Elaine is this kind of friend to me. I can't imagine her dead. I don't want to.

I arrived at Elaine's door one early December afternoon to find her wrestling with a roll of Scotch tape and a wide red ribbon. "I'm no good at this!" she said to me, "But they're giving me trouble for not decorating my door."

"Who's 'they'?" I asked.

"I don't know," she said, and then pushed her face close and asked, "Are you 'they'?"

"Heavens no!" I said, "I'd never get on someone's case for not doing Christmas decorating. You should see my house."

She pulled me inside, into her sitting room where she knelt before a wooden writing desk, pulling out drawers and files, talking about a poem she wanted to show me. "Just to see what you think," she said. After much searching, she found it, holding it triumphantly aloft. It had been laboriously typed on heavy yellow-gold paper, and was titled "Thanatopsis", by William Cullen Bryant. She sent me home with her only copy.

Translated, the title meant "Meditation upon Death". I read it all, bumping somewhat uncomfortably through the older English, while appreciating also its depth and rich vocabulary. Its subject matter had me uneasy, yet I was fascinated. It was a striking poem, a haunting poem, full of love for nature, life and beauty, all the while regarding the inevitable death of living things with a speculative and unflinching eye. The writer – only

17 years old when he set it down – had apparently returned to the poem seven years later to add a final stanza, giving warmth to what I found to be a rather cerebral approach. When I returned to Elaine's suite a week later, yellow-gold paper in hand, the stanza I read aloud to her was this last one:

> *So live, that when thy summons comes to join*
> *The innumerable caravan... where each shall take*
> *His chamber in the silent halls of death,*
> *Thou go not, like the quarry-slave at night,*
> *Scourged to his dungeon, but sustained and soothed*
> *By an unfaltering trust, approach thy grave*
> *Like one who wraps the drapery of his couch*
> *About him, and lies down to pleasant dreams.*[1]

"Does this poem comfort you?" I asked Elaine. "Yes," she said, and told me that she had read that last stanza at her husband's funeral, and that she believed he had died with such 'unfaltering trust'.

Elaine is uncommon in many ways - her energy, her awareness of and care for others, her ability to brighten any gathering. Particularly compelling for me is her continual belief in the goodness of life, even at the age of 85. It's not a point of view frequently encountered in the retirement community context. I don't know how many times I've heard elders say, "Why they call this the golden years is beyond me!" - and, I confess, it's a point of view I rarely find within myself. Elaine, however, believes (seemingly with minimal effort) that her life is indeed in a golden phase. When I expressed surprise at her comment, Elaine responded in typical fashion, with a mixture of honesty and pragmatism.

"I've just been fortunate," she said to me. Her sitting room windows were large, and overlooked her deck, which, at that moment, was overrun with birds. "The experiences in my life have basically been very good. Now, someone else who's spent years in a prison camp or a concentration camp, or been abused – their attitude's going to be quite different, isn't it? So, I can't take credit for what I am. I am only living out of what life has dealt - and it has given goodness to me." Elaine pointed out the window, "It's just like that - look, isn't it great? - it's just like that little chickadee finding the seed right there in the feeder. Flying back and forth from the tree, he says, 'life is good - I just have to step out, fly off the branch and there it is.' I've been fortunate like that. You think my attitude is exceptional, but I don't think it is."

"Well, that's rare too - being grateful and able to recognize when life is good." I said.

"Good," said Elaine, "it's heavenly! At times I do think, 'Elaine, you don't project far enough ahead, you should be thinking about what the future holds.' But my future is the moment. And I'm not going to worry if the doctor should say to me, 'You've got terminal this or that.' I'll think, 'Well, this is part of the package,' and it will be interesting to see what that journey is all about. It's a curiosity."

One day, I spoke openly to Elaine about my experience of living on my own, far from my family. I spoke of one relative who did live nearby, someone I could ask to pick me up if my car broke down, or to housesit - even cat sit. No gift or fee was necessary – just a simple thank-you, and the knowledge that I would readily reciprocate when a similar need arose for him. That was 'family': you could, on some level, ask a lot - even take advantage of each other. Now this relative was talking of moving, leaving town, and I found myself nonplussed, grieving, bereft. When I told Elaine how surprised I was at the depth of emotion and loss that had arisen, she listened quietly, and then said, "I'm sad you feel that way - you shouldn't have to feel that way." I was surprised by the strength of her response. 'Well that's okay Elaine, that's just life," I began. "No, it's not," said Elaine, "It's not the way it's meant to be. You're not meant to be alone like that." She set down her coffee cup and turned to face me. "I could be your friend like that," said Elaine, "You can bring your cat here anytime. I could be family for you...oh, but you probably think I'm too old."

I didn't know how to respond. The generosity and power of what Elaine had offered was quite overwhelming. What would it mean to be that kind of a friend with someone who was 35 years older than me? It was a time stretch that I had never considered. Certainly, in a friendship with someone in their 80's, the spectre of loss is very real. I rolled it over in my mind for days. I knew I was already very attached to Elaine, and felt she was trustworthy, honest, and good. I felt also that I wanted to learn from her this one thing, this thing I couldn't seem to learn on my own – that life is good, simply that. Despite the risk of loss, despite the risk of loving. I wanted to be the chickadee taking that seed from the feeder outside her window, freely trusting in the goodness of the moment.

Later, in my own 'digs' that night, I watched the birds fly from tree to tree through my back window. I knew I could say 'no' to Elaine's offer of deepening friendship, and I knew also that she would accept my choice as surely as a bird accepts flight, that mystery of one air current or another beneath its wings. But, I reasoned, why hide from Elaine when goodness awaits, for the moment, or for the season? I remembered another stanza from the poem, "Yet a few days, and thee the all-beholding sun shall see no more." Who was I kidding, anyway? Clearly, the poem was as much about how to live as it was about death.

In the midst of this mental wrestle, I had to grin. I knew what Elaine would have to say if she were sitting across from me – "You're getting too analytical, Melody", she'd say. "Just let it all go – put it in a pot and let it simmer. Let it go, and just *live*!"

And so, I've done just that. And while that pot simmers, our visits continue, rich, unscripted, and good. Elaine surprises and blesses me with her friendship - we talk about our shared love of the things of earth, while the birds flit back and forth from the trees to the liberally-filled feeders on her deck. In one way, she is a comfort and a balm to me, the mentor I always wanted. She is helping me learn to face life, and death, with 'unfaltering trust'. In another, we are like two girl cousins, ageless, lying on our backs in a field somewhere, under a summer sky so blue you could swim in it, sunk into the inarticulate bosom of nature, the earth that bore us, and one day will again take us in.

And so, like a field wishing to be covered in beauty, in green and growing things, I invite Elaine to tread upon me with her stories and wisdom, to be the farmer and the plough so we can grow life's goodness together. And when the day comes – if it is not first to me – and the farmer does not return, I suppose I shall lie fallow, ever-willing and infinitely patient as the earth, for some hopping and bright-eyed bird to drop its seeds into my heart.

Winter solace

*I*t was a mid-December afternoon, one of those sombre winter days of brief light that must be endured before Solstice arrives with the promise of longer days. The weather experts predicted it was about to turn cold – uncharacteristically cold, at least for B.C.'s Lower Mainland. Snow was coming, and high winds, bringing the temperature with wind chill to a potential minus 20 degrees Celsius. Our community became a hive of activity and preparation. Cars were all safely parked in the heated underground, and the staff made plans for snow shovelling or heating issues that might arise. Like animals preparing for winter, we all felt there was something more we should be doing. Later that afternoon, as I walked down the hall at Hallmark, it seemed that indeed, many were following the lead of the animals and simply holing up; it was uncommonly - almost eerily - quiet, not a soul to be seen.

As I rounded the corner, an icy wind blew into the hallway from a suite with its door propped open. I slowed, and glanced inside to make sure everything was all right. The sliding door to the outside patio was pushed open and a pink-cheeked Juliette, one of our newer residents, could be seen dragging a large rectangular wooden box of geraniums in from the deck. Smiling, she waved me in. "Supposed to snow," she said, huffing, and I helped her carry the box inside; it was long, heavy and unwieldy. Juliette's face held an expression of weary, strong resolve. "You look like you're on a mission," I observed. She gestured towards several other potted plants still out on the deck, beneath a thickening steel grey sky. "I'm trying to beat the cold, at least for some of them," she said; "they'll never last out there." "Will you keep them in your living room?" I asked. "No," she said, smiling, "I'm going to decorate my parking spot for Christmas. I think I can just find room for these two boxes." "I'll help you carry them down," I said.

"Such a pity to lose your beautiful flowers," I remarked, for Juliette's deck was filled with them. They looked particularly fragile, as if huddled together in the cold. "There's a season for everything," said Juliette, taking a firmer grip on her end of the box, and leading the way to the elevator. The pungent smell of geraniums filled the elevator as we plunged down towards the underground parking level. "I needed a project today," said Juliette. She told me that a close friend had died only a few days before. "He lived just down the hall from me," she said. "It's so sad, so hard, and such a shock. You're never prepared for it." The elevator doors opened. "I need to keep busy," she said, "or it's all I'll think about.

We set the geraniums down in front of her car in the parking stall, bright green leaves bobbing and strangely laid bare against the stretch of pocked grey cement. "They may not survive here either, who knows?" she said, looking at them sadly; "but I have to try." We turned and walked back toward the elevator. "And of course," she said, "when something like this – like my friend - happens, it makes you think of your own…"

Her voice trailed off. She looked at me meaningfully. "'Your own death?" I said, speaking the obvious, wanting to clear the air, open the curtains, fling open the windows to what was wanting to be said. "Yes," she said, exhaling. She looked at me with what I perceived as gratefulness, and drew off her stiff cotton gardening gloves with bits of dirt and bright poppyred petals still clinging to them. "Where there is life, how can there not be death?"

"And, in this place," she said, pushing the elevator button to go back up, "the two live together a little too close for comfort."   As the elevator door opened to her floor, I saw we'd left a trail: bits of moss and hot red geranium petals scattered on the rug behind us, bright clues, harbingers of relentless spring.

Tickers and geraniums

I was walking down the park trail that borders both Hallmarks one afternoon, and saw a familiar figure standing beside the path. It was Juliette. I quickened my step. She was such a pleasure to be with, with an ability to soothe and smooth life's difficulties, while at the same time still being honest about it, lifting her paw over the truth and touching the surface of that water as delicately as would a cat, to see where it began and ended.

And today the water of the small lake in the park revealed itself clear and beautiful, sparkling with light. Juliette was standing at the side of the path, one hand braced against her lower back, huffing slightly. "Just have to get my breath back," she said, smiling her welcome at me. "My ticker needs to slow down."

I glimpsed once again the contrast between the aging body and the ageless soul. For while her body was clearly paining her, Juliette's eyes were sparkling like everyone else's on the path that day. It was spring, finally spring, after an uncommonly long winter. The sun was brilliant, warming all but the well-shaded edges of the path; buds were fat and green - near to bursting - and the odd tree had already begun to leaf out.

I told Juliette that I'd written a story about "our geraniums in the underground parking lot" experience. I hoped the reference to that time of her friend's death wouldn't pain her too much. Her eyes shone, though for a moment there was a ruffle, like on the surface of a pond when a brief cold wind blows. "Are they still blooming?" I asked hopefully, naively; "those geraniums we took downstairs before the storm - did they survive?" "Oh no, they're not blooming," replied Juliette; "they're all brown; I didn't water them." My heart fell just a little, as I chastised myself for my child's hope about things, for wanting a world where all is well. "But they'll come back, of course," she said, smiling at my dismay. "Once I prune them down" – she made a pinching gesture with her fingers - "and take off all the dead leaves, and put them outside again, they'll come back." "Really," I said, lamely, reverently; "I didn't know that about geraniums." "Oh yes," she said, "I've had geraniums come back as big as a shrub sometimes – as long as they don't freeze."

I continued on down the path, while Juliette turned towards home. It had been my grandmother who knew about flowers in my family. She'd tended them every season, year after year, decade after decade. I remembered her room full of flowers in pots, crowded on old wooden shelves in the back of her house. I guess she too had stored her plants for the winter: geraniums, African violets, all manner of flowers whose names I'd either forgotten, or never known in the first place. The smell in that back room had been sharp and pungent - yet I found it cleansed my mind somehow, swept away the old like brown dried leaves to reveal the peppery wet smell of earth, that spring smell of life awakening. That slightly offensive, slightly beautiful essence of life had burrowed into the cracks and crevices of my grandmother's fingers after she'd snapped the brown stems from her geraniums, and now it nestled as real and vivid in the cracks and crevices of my own memory - a brave green shoot coming up through damp and crumbled earth.

I had always loved the idea of geraniums: as an artist their bright colors; as a writer, the stories and memories they evoked because of my grandmother's love for them. In my own life, I hadn't had much luck with tending flowers. Just that past summer, I had bought a geranium, but in that unseasonably cold winter, it had died. Unlike Juliette, I had not brought it inside for winter. And so I expect I'll join the hordes of spring shoppers at the garden store, buying a fresh new one, and trying again. For me, the knowledge that comes from tending the earth, year after year, decade after decade, is simply not there.

I imagine what I had learned from Juliette would have been common knowledge to the average gardener. But I was dazzled. How could a plant, long dried and still – unwatered, unlighted – be brought back to life, simply by restoring those two elements? I walked on, amazed at this mystery. Did anyone else feel a shudder under their feet? Or was I one of few who just didn't know about this secret life of plants, and thus hadn't become inured to it? Who can see the world uncovered like this and remain unchanged, or say the word 'spring' without falling to the earth themselves, into this life fuelled by a force far beyond our understanding?

Did that knowledge inform Juliette, I wondered, as she stood alongside the path, waiting for her ticker to catch up? Had it informed my grandmother also, as she faced the challenges of her life?

And so it is, that last winter's writing about Juliette's geraniums, that I'd laid to rest with its note of finality - enclosed in a story – has now opened up again, opened into possibility like a quieted and brown geranium comes to life again after a long hard winter. It opens up with as much possibility as the season of spring offers us all – faltering or light-footed or aging. The cat touching the skin of the water, the silent fish shadowing the bottom of the pond, the dogs diligently marking their existence along the path. The Canada Geese arching their necks, hissing at us when we walk by, or, fully indifferent, snatching at bits of grass, leaving their leavings, and waddling on. This was spring. We were walking in it - we *were* it somehow - that is, if we so chose to be.

I turned down the path to the car, and caught a glimpse of Juliette on the final leg of her walk home. She stood, hand on her back, watching the lake. Patiently waiting for her ticker to subside, so she could continue walking. Into this broad and amazing world of spring, the blind trust of the forward push, the wakening into light.

Sam and the music

I love music," said Sam to me one day, eyes cast to the ground as though confessing something shameful; "I have always loved music." Hymns, as it turned out, were his favourite. "But I can't sing them," said Sam with a note of finality in his voice; "I can't hold a tune to save my life." He probably saw in my face that I wasn't convinced. "My aunts always told me to shut up because I ruined everything when I sang." he said. "Your aunts aren't here," I reminded him gently, "and I'd venture to say that most of us in this room couldn't hold a tune to save our lives! Maybe you're not as bad as you think you are."

Sam didn't buy my logic. Still, as the weeks passed, he began to show up for the community's hymn sing – well, if sitting in a chair nearest the exit, and as far away as possible from where the hymns were being sung, could be counted as "showing up". In those early days, he worked quite deliberately, I thought, to appear as disengaged from the gathering as he could. It was as though he wanted his presence to be seen as happenstance, as though he was only there for a moment, or waiting for a ride to go somewhere much more important than a mere hymn sing.

After his stroke, a new and pure intent began to emerge, a crack in the shell that kept Sam from moving out into the world. It didn't take long before that shell was gone, cracked and fallen like a robin's eggshell on a spring path. Soon it was Sam sitting in the back row of chairs that surrounded the hymn sing – a great advancement for him. From month to month, his seating choice progressed forward, until he settled in somewhere in the middle, where he would sit, rapt as a baby bird, gulping back his emotion at the sweetness of the food now offered him, food he'd never dared to partake of before.

It was wonderful to see him, that first time, up and dancing at our spring gala. Initially, he'd retreated once more to the seat furthest away, his one slippered foot tapping awkwardly as he watched those who had braved the dance floor. He may have thought himself invisible, but his longing to join in emanated from him as vividly as daylight. His first response to my invitation was "But I can't dance." "I can't dance either, Sam," I told him, "We'll just step back and forth to the music, that'll be good enough. And we'll stay here at the back."

Those translucent blue eggshells lay beautiful now, forgotten on the ground behind him. They were beautiful because they had held Sam, and broken because they had encased him. Now it was time for Sam – old Sam, teetering-on-the-end-of-his-life-Sam - like every other baby bird, to start to fly.

Pioneering community

/ 've lived at Hallmark for almost ten years!"
Frances announced to me in the middle of
one of our Christmas galas. She was seated at the head
of a white-clothed table in Hallmark Square, a room
festooned with Christmas lights and decorations. Her
guests had gone home, and Frances was enjoying the last
of the live entertainer's songs from the fifties to the
seventies, punctuated by Elvis-style renditions of
Christmas carols.

Finished with helping to serve the meal, and
having re-set the dining room for the next day, I'd
crossed the festively decorated Square to sit next to
Frances. She'd been among the first residents to move
in when Hallmark's first building opened, and had

quickly taken ownership of her role as pioneer and advisor.

Frances recalled her first conversation with one of Hallmark's owners. "Stan told me right away when he met me, 'You'll be on our resident council!'" she said to me. I jumped a little in my chair; her powerful voice readily trumped the music. "He didn't even know me; I guess he must've heard about me from somewhere." She smiled triumphantly. "I've been involved for many years, you know, in the community." Yes, I was aware of her community work – good work - sometimes she held her committee meetings at Hallmark. It was inspiring to have someone engaged and doing the hard work of leadership, and Frances seemed up to the task.

My mind returned to the early days of Hallmark's opening, and Frances coming into my office with varied requests; although they often came across as orders. Turns out Frances had been in the army, and no doubt that was where she had learned her decisive and direct style of delivery. Frances wanted issues resolved quickly and, I'm sure, often found my own leadership style frustrating. Not that I really had a style at that point – I was new to my role, and admittedly uncertain. I was however, keenly aware that we were establishing a culture, and that each decision was precedent-setting. And so, it took time for me to arrive at decisions, to consider the many facets of this diamond-in-the-rough community.

Frances's suite overlooked the front of the building. This offered her full visual command of the comings and goings of the community. Office visits from Frances brought forth clear recommendations on how to handle everything from idling cars to those who smoked. When cars passed the front door of Hallmark on the way to the parking lot at a rate of speed deemed too fast, Frances suggested we post a digital speed readout near the entrance, so that people could see how fast they were going. "Who would monitor it?" I asked. "I'd be happy to!" said Frances. In the end, we gained Frances' reluctant blessing on a roadside sign that read, "Drive with care; Grandparents crossing". Most of the time, Frances and I were able to come to terms with our differences in approach; it was clear that we both cared about this community, and had chosen to make it our own.

Years passed. I left my role as Executive Director, and moved into the Corporate Office, thereby not as involved in the daily workings of Hallmark as before. Frances completed her terms as Chair of Hallmark's Resident Council, and focused on her committee work in the broader community. When our second retirement residence was built, she moved over, indicating that she wasn't in need of all of the services in the first building. She was the first to move into this building; Frances thrived on being a pioneer.

The second building, however, was full of more independent residents, whose version of community often included outside activities, family, and friends. They went out often, and the need for an internal Resident Council just didn't surface. Over the years, Frances chose to spend more time in her suite. "The TV is my babysitter now," she told me ruefully one day.

As we sat together at the Gala these many years later, Frances recounted to me how her first husband had died when she was 34. "I went to work right away; I was left with four children and not 2 pennies to rub together." She married again at 60, and her second husband died six years later. My interest quickened; I told her that I was just beginning a life on my own. "It is possible to be content and live alone – I did it," she offered proudly. Then, with some surprise, she said, "I've been a widow for 44 years!" She paused a moment, recalculating – "Yes, 44 years, if you count from the first time till now, minus those 6 years married in between." I asked her, "If you were asked to share what you've learned with other women living alone, what would you say?" Frances responded without hesitation. "I'd say, 'be involved in things, don't just stay home'. And I'd say, 'be content'."

I commented on the tenacity and toughness that had brought her through her difficulties, and the great store of courage she would have had to draw upon. She responded, "I used to be afraid of my own shadow – I was tall, and in my mind, not as attractive as my sister." I was quiet for a moment, trying to imagine Frances afraid. As if reading my thoughts, Frances continued. "It was because of my upbringing that I was able to manage all those years alone," she said. "It was the example of my parents. My father helped me stand tall and be proud of my height." Her face glowed with love for her parents and, I thought, with a well-earned sense of personal accomplishment.

That conversation was powerful for me. Neither Frances nor I felt the need to solve or fix anything. We were just two women living on our own, sharing our stories. It was an unusual way for Frances and me to relate, and an unexpected gift.

Given the familiarity of our conversation that evening, I wondered if my relationship with Frances would change, if there would be a difference in our interactions from then on. The answer to that became clear the next day, when I saw Frances coming out of the dining room. Her "Good day, Melody" had the same firm, direct tone she'd always had. She offered no more softness, though I'd thought she might, given our mutual vulnerabilities of the night before. No, Frances was still

Frances, and always would be. She had earned her stripes, fair and square, and was not about to become sentimental about any of it, or surrender her territory that was so hard-won. A hard life, but an undivided life. Who would not wish for the same?

Frances had taken her challenges and turned them into a powerful voice, a force willing to work hard for community, something she knew women like herself needed. A place to do their work. To turn straw into gold.

....

One morning, a few months later, I realized that I hadn't seen much of Frances over the last while, and stopped by her suite to say hello. She said, "I know I'm not contributing like I have in the past. These days, I'm just content with my phone calls and my children." She had a note of apology in her voice. I wondered aloud if 'just being contented' could in itself be a significant and rare contribution, asking, "Frances, how many people do you know in our present culture who are truly content?"

I pondered our conversation for several days afterward. It made me wonder about the unseen influence that ripples out from each person - like a stretch of water between us, impressionable, responsive. Might Frances be giving yet another gift to the community surrounding her? As her waters still to contentment, do they mirror another, more profound light?

Holy ground, sometimes

My first encounter with Charlie was at a housewarming lunch at Hallmark. His wife had died recently, and he sat silently at the table and wept through most of the meal. His daughter sat beside him, quiet and supportive; you could feel her strength, and her love for her father. Despite Charlie's tears, an ultimate stoicism seemed to emanate from them both – an inner metal enabling them to survive. It seemed a familial thing, like those Scottish crests that families carry. The words around the Dunlop emblem, I imagined, could read, "Take life as it comes – and keep going".

Over time, we learned more about Charlie's life; how he, at the age of 17, joined the Canadian army. "I told them a fib; I told them I was 18," he said, grinning.

One day, when I asked Charlie why he had made that choice, he looked straight at me, and said, "For the money." He didn't elaborate or try to justify his decision, just left it out on the table as it was.

"I was in the Special Forces for five years," said Charlie. "We cleaned up what nobody else wanted to clean up. After that, it was twenty-five more years in the army, doing the same thing – jumping out of airplanes and shooting people." He was quiet for a moment. Then he grinned, "First time I jumped out of an airplane, I peed myself."

Charlie was born and grew up on Vancouver Island, an island I know as lush and green, with that wonderful tranquil indolence that seems to pervade island living. At the age of 17, from delivering newspapers, he was plunged into the harsh world of war.

The First Special Service Force (FSSF) - the unique combat unit in which Charlie spent his early army years - was made up of elite Canadian and American fighters. "When I first joined the Army, I was in the Canadian Scottish," said Charlie. "Then they formed the First Special Service Force, and I volunteered, not expecting to go, but they accepted me. My understanding at that time was that the Special Services was better than the normal infantry, better than the airborne; it was a combination of both put together. And it *was* good – they taught us a different way to fight.

I can laugh at it now," Charlie mused, "but then I couldn't. I was scared to death - my buddy and myself both were - but we did the job anyway."

"We lost lots of people, but that was war. What I couldn't bear," said Charlie, "was seeing the way children and women were treated - maimed. I couldn't bear that. And nothing was done to help them. I can still remember picking up kids this size" – he held his hands shoulder-width apart – "and tears were coming out of my eyes faster than I could do it. And the Commander came over and asked, 'What's your problem Charlie?' and I says 'that', and pointed at the pile of young kids. They weren't all dead, but injured. I said, 'We're partially responsible for this, and so's the enemy. Can't we find another way to settle this?'"

While Charlie's description of this scenario was incomplete, I didn't question him further. Instead, I tried to imagine a 17-year-old, catapulted into the uncommon expectations of the Special Service Force. Referred to as 'shock troops', its members often raided strategic positions and parachuted behind enemy lines. Training in hand-to-hand combat and explosives was part of the program, and since the men often had to dispose of the enemy silently, they were skilled with a thin-bladed knife called a V-42. The small units, with faces and weapons blackened, would skilfully overwhelm German defences, and then disappear into the night, earning them the name found in a German officer's personal diary "die schwarzen Teufeln" (the Black Devils).

"I think the worst time of my life in the army was in Italy when we ..." There was a pause as Charlie fought for the right word. "When we *freed* an orphanage. It was staffed with Italians who were part German. My commander said, 'well they're our enemy, do something about it.' So we did." said Charlie. His laugh was short, forced, almost a bark; he blew his nose. The air was thick, and we sat in silence for a time. I surmised that, in this case, Charlie's unit had had to "dispose" of the staff, but didn't feel comfortable asking him about it.

"Yeah," said Charlie, finally breaking the silence, "Wars don't prove a damn thing other than they kill a lot of people. Other than that, they prove nothing. One of them's going to be a winner and one going to be a loser, but in the long run, they're both losers. There's no warning that you're going to do something to the enemy, they just tell you, and you just do it. Oh, but when you get to be in your 20's and you start to think, that's dangerous for the higher-ups. One day the Company Sergeant Major called me over, and said, 'Dunlop, come over here!' He said, 'I want you to go over, take that man into a tent and have a talk with him.' I said, 'What the hell's he doing wrong, sir?' He said, 'He's moaning.' I said, 'Well, that's allowed.' 'Not with him, no. He's moaning about what we're doing here. He's going to bugger up the whole system." Charlie's description of their hour-long conversation showed how he had survived his experiences of war. "Think of today, not yesterday or the day before, *today*," he'd told his tormented comrade. "You're thinking about what happened yesterday, and that can't possibly affect you positively. So think about now - only now."

"War makes no sense and it doesn't solve anything," continued Charlie. "Never has and never will. Because mankind - and I say this from my heart and my mind – has not learned how to live with each other. No complications to it. They just want to fight, and when they get fighting and hurt each other, they wonder why. They're not just thick in the head, they're cuckoo."

"Still, we had fun, too," said Charlie then, leaning back in his chair, smiling slightly, "we had fun."

"We had a major that was an idiot, and we put up with him for three months. Finally my buddy and I got together, crept into his tent one night and tied his bootlaces together, then went outside and rang the gong. All we heard was 'swish' and 'crash'! Anyway the next day he got me and my buddy, and said 'I know that you two are guilty.' I said, 'You can't say that sir, you have no proof.' He said, 'The only proof I need is looking at your face!' Then I told him, 'If you'd smarten up, we'd leave you alone.' Oh, some of them were good leaders, but some were awful - couldn't lead you to the potty, let alone to the front."

I asked Charlie if there was a Commander who was memorable to him, someone he trusted. "Oh yes," said Charlie, "Fredericks. Because 99% of the time in the unit, we were scared to death - this thing was going a mile a minute - and he'd go up and down the line talking to us. He'd say, 'You're scared, aren't you?' When he'd ask me that, I'd say, 'Is it noticeable?' He'd say, 'Yes.' So I'd say, 'Then yes, I am.'"

"Humour is good," I said. "Oh, yes," said Charlie. "Beats the hell out of crying."

"You know what I think should happen?" Charlie asked, "I think that Canada and the United States should form one army, to enforce world peace." I laughed, "Isn't that ironic, that an army must enforce world peace?" "Yes," said Charlie, his gaze burning into mine. "But that's the only way it's going to happen." 'What do I know?' I thought. I am a child of peace - I have known nothing else. War to me is a story, a picture on TV, something that happens in other lands. This is due to the work of people like Charlie, from whom life drew out their mettle, forged it, and hammered it fine. It was unsettling at times to look at Charlie's face. You didn't know who you were going to see – the well-loved boy from the Island, the husband and father, or the man who obeyed orders, and jumped out of airplanes to shoot people.

Charlie said that while he was at war, he wrote to his family every six months or so. "I wrote to my dad one day and said, 'I'm still your son, I still respect you, but unfortunately I'm in the war doing this stupid job.' And my father, who had been in the First World War, wrote back and said 'You're right.' When I did come home from overseas, I went to visit him, and you'd have thought I'd never left home." Charlie's voice dropped into tenderness as he made the gesture of his father hugging him. "Oh, God," he said, and sat quiet for a time. "Any man that can't cry, there's something wrong with him."

"When the war ended and I came back to Canada, I went back to the regular force. It was totally different." Charlie paused, studying the backs of his hands laid upon the table. "I'm lucky to be here. Because some of the things I did, I'm not proud of."

I wondered how he'd made peace with himself, with all the lives broken and taken away. He didn't try to help me understand more of what his life had been. He had said what he needed to; now he simply stood there, as though holding the gleaming metal of a gun barrel smooth, polished and ready for battle. He didn't like it, but it was what he had been told to do. And so, it got done. That was Charlie.

I didn't know what to say to Charlie. My words didn't have the strength that his had, even though his were few, and often coarse, and frightening. There are men like him all over the world, who have paid the price of war and peace – both above and below the earth.

I'd found that when Charlie spoke about his war experiences, it was often in understatement. Was it to protect me, I wondered, or himself? Was his memory of that time fading? Whatever the reason, I did not push for more information. Who was I, for the sake of my own comprehension, to push him back into those intense experiences? Writing life isn't like writing fiction – you don't necessarily have the whole picture, all the 'threads' to be pulled into a resolved, whole cloth. There are some things that simply remain beyond us.

While I cannot fathom Charlie's experience, still I want to record something of it - it feels like holy ground sometimes. What this man went through, what he saw, would darken the most courageous soul, and yet here he is, tough as nails, sitting across from me. I feel like I should take my shoes off. How he and many like him, have suffered. There is a beauty in the room as he speaks; he curbs his language, shortens the details of his stories, I think, to spare me - I who can't even bear to watch movies about war. And yet, we sit together in the same world, Charlie and I. Inexplicable.

Charlie has lived at Hallmark for several years now. In the summers, he's a golf pro. "Come warmer weather," he says, "I'll be on the driving range, and any people who want help, they've got it. Doesn't cost them a damn thing, just a coffee."

I was told of a conversation in which Stan, an owner of Hallmark, thanked Charlie for the way he was helping in the community – bringing other residents their walkers, giving them rides to doctors' appointments, etc. Charlie had fixed Stan with an unwavering gaze and said, "Well, I was such a miserable bastard in the old days, I'm just trying to do something good before it's all over."

I wonder if Charlie ever wonders what his life might have been if he had been born in a time of peace. Conversely, do I wonder what my life would have been if I had been born in a time of war? How do we fathom each other's lives, each other's experiences, when they are so utterly different; how do we extend understanding to each other when we do not understand? Somewhere, buried in that impossible question, that impossible necessity, is the seed of peace.

Never too old

*H*ugh and I got into the elevator one grey Monday morning and as we stood facing forward, the elevator doors closed. When they snapped shut, he turned to me and exclaimed, "Alone at last!" I laughed, of course, what else could I do? Hugh was 93 years old, and I a mere forty. For Hugh, age clearly didn't matter.

Hugh was a regular at what we called 'the stud table', a table at the edge of the dining room where four single male residents dined every day. Hugh paid little or no attention to the physical wear and tear his physical self bore after decades of living. Hugh was spirited, pure and simple, and that spirit shone forth daily in his choices, conversations and activities. He had a way about him, charming and sincere, a way of lifting the spirits of those around him, particularly women. For many female staff at Hallmark, upon greeting Hugh with the typical "How are you today?" were met with a joyful wink and "The better for seeing you!" Although we knew that Hugh repeated this response to many others, in that moment it felt great; it felt like a safe flirt. What was it to Hugh? We chose not to ask.

"I fascinate you - what good does that do me?" Hugh asked me one day. Again, I laughed; Hugh lived out, on a daily basis, his fascination for life, and for learning. "I'm very interested in DNA," he said to me one day. "I've tried to find out how they do it - take a sample, put it on a special machine, and then get a profile and all the gene arrangements. I've looked it up on the 'net, but haven't had any luck yet." He was also trying to understand the mysteries of vision. "So I went to the specialist," said Hugh, "and asked him, 'Can you tell me how we see?' And he started talking about the optic nerve and all that kind of thing, and when he was done, I said, 'Yes, but can you tell me how it is that we *see*?' And he said, 'I don't know, Hugh, I can't answer that question.'" Hugh looked at me then, "And what's it got to do with DNA?" he asked.

Undeterred, Hugh moved from one question to another. He was studying Russian – after already learning French, Italian and Greek (although he said he'd forgotten much of what he knew). And Hugh didn't just want to learn to speak Russian, he also wanted to know about how the language developed. "The alphabet is thirty-three letters – the whole thing is crazy! I tried to track it down; the Slovaks are where it came from, and a bit from the Greeks…and then the Hebrews got into it. It's a case of trying to find out how it all works."

When I asked him why he was still so full of life at 92, Hugh replied, "I just carry on from day to day, that's all. I take my pills, go downstairs for breakfast, get in a little trouble…"

Hugh and his walking stick were a familiar sight to the residents of Princess Street. He walked for about thirty minutes every morning. His mind, too, was always on the go. "When I have nothing on my mind, I invent a situation and try to solve it. I have these stories that keep running around in my mind." He laughed, "I'm the protagonist who always tells the characters what to do."

"I'll tell you what suits me," said Hugh one day. "I don't have much furniture in my suite – it's almost monastic – and I sit in my chair and look out the window there, and I watch the leaves move back and forth. I think about all that sap and carbon dioxide; I think – they're cutting down these trees and that'll be very bad for us, we need oxygen." He sat for a moment, concentrating on something I didn't see. "I feel like I'm on an airship that's going someplace," he mused. "I don't know where it's going, but I'm very interested in what the pilot is doing. That's the way it is for me."

Hugh looked at me intently, "I tell people 'whatever you're most interested in, pursue it! Find out what you want to do, and do it with all your might.' Me, I'd like to go to school again."

As Hugh left the room, he caught sight of himself in a mirror on the wall. It stopped him short. "Who's that old man?" he asked, startled. "Guess I have to stay out of the way of mirrors!"

One day, just for fun, we asked Hallmark residents how old they *felt*, as opposed to their actual physical age. The results were astonishing. Most of them felt as though they were between the ages of twenty and thirty-five. I can't for the life of me remember Hugh's answer to that question – was he the one who'd said 'seventeen'? Or, who knows, his knees may have been bothering him that day, and so he'd felt his physiological age. In the end, I suppose it doesn't really matter what he said. Hugh only knew one way to live. Hugh was ageless.

From taxi driver to millionaire

*O*ne of our new residents brought her friend Bill to the community housewarming luncheon. He sat beside me, and immediately I sensed him to be honest and solid as a rock – a man without artifice. Though I had been to these monthly luncheons for close to a decade and had heard many stories, this one stayed vivid in my mind for days.

Bill dropped directly and without hesitation into the essence of his story like a rock dropped into the center of a pond. He told us that, even as a boy, he'd known what God wanted him to be – a minister – but he also knew he didn't want to be one. All the ministers he'd known in his Southern Manitoba community had been very poor, and he intended to be a millionaire. So Bill lived what he called his "no" for a long time.

Ironically, he married a woman whose family had "groomed her to marry a minister". She was a beautiful soloist, Bill said, and they were most disappointed by her choice of a mate. Having no idea of the calling placed within him, her family didn't come to the wedding. Bill and his wife began their life together in Winnipeg, where he drove taxi; he then began a successful business. His perseverance and hard work seemed to be paying off, with his goal of great wealth almost within reach. Bill paused for a moment; his eyes searched the room. "But I took to drinking," he said matter-of-factly, his voice quieter, "and lost it all." The devastation of the whole experience drove him literally to his knees, and he and his wife began to attend church. At the end of one service there was an altar call, and his wife turned to him and said, "Shall we go?" "I thought she meant 'go' as in 'leaving, *outside*'", Bill said, "so I said 'yes', and stood up. But it turned out," he laughed, "that she meant 'go' as in '*forward*.'"

And so it was that Bill began to allow the voice of God to change and direct him. One day, when he was praying, he heard God's voice clearly in his head: "Now I want you to train for the ministry." "I can't do that," Bill replied, "We have no money." For indeed they were very poor, and by then there were children to support. But back came the voice without hesitation: "If I send, I provide." And so, Bill applied to Bible College.

Just two weeks into his studies, one of the teachers approached him and said, "I need you to preach at a small new church this Sunday – just over 30 people. Will you come?" By this time, Bill was learning not to argue. So he did, and, lo and behold they asked him back the next Sunday, and then the next. Bill modestly attributed the repeated invitations to his wife's beautiful singing, and his son's accordion playing, but it must have been more than that. He stayed on as their pastor until they needed one full-time – he couldn't fulfill those duties because he was still studying.

As Bill continued to share his story with us all these years later, I sat to the left of him, watching with an artist's fascination the strength in his face, the relaxed yet controlled way his jaw lifted and dropped and formed the words that told us his life, his heart. I felt a yearning to hear more of his knowledge of God; I wanted to be in his congregation. He spoke of how he and his wife, at the age of 49, had chosen to adopt a baby, and how this little girl had become the greatest gift of his life. And I wanted to be that little girl; I wanted to be his daughter, chosen and beloved; I wanted to be adopted by this man of God, this silent humble and real father who didn't mind a bit of humanity in those around him, and who was unafraid to share his own.

And so it was that I sat beside a man with a heart of gold. Did he know he'd become a millionaire?

Travel light, travel far

*O*live was a mysterious figure to me. Even though we both were part of a rather intense pioneering service trip to Guatemala, my sense of who she was remained vague. While the rest of us laughed, wept, connected and struggled in the crucible of a new culture, new companions and the raw realities of life within Guatemala, Olive remained her usual self: regal, self-contained and polite. She pleasantly addressed the needs of the moment, nothing more. I found her baffling. I found her intriguing.

Throughout that trip, Olive asked little for herself. Other than her consistent quest at dinner for a glass of Guatemalan wine (finally an English-speaking waiter informed us that Guatemala did not make its own wine - a visible disappointment for Olive), and sometimes borrowing clothes from other team members. One hot day, Olive borrowed summer shorts from one of the male members of the group; while they were large on her, fluttering gently like wings about her thin legs, she was quite unconcerned about appearance, and ultimately practical, happy to have something cool to wear.

Snapshot: *Olive didn't carry more than she needed. She travelled light – emotionally and physically. Olive also saw no point in going to a museum. "Why would you revisit the past?" she'd ask, "That's done, that's over, that's history." She spent no time worrying about the future either. When she made up her mind, there was no second-guessing. When you travelled light, you could travel far.* (Dawna, wife of Olive's nephew)

Looking back, the most personal glimpse I had of Olive was at the trip's outset. We'd missed our connection in Florida en route to Guatemala, and a group of us went for a walk at dusk near our hotel. Olive and I walked together for a time, and she confided in me an apprehension about the upcoming trip. "I'm not comfortable with babies and small children," she said, as she knew a good portion of time would be spent at an orphanage and small school for children of lean economic means. "I'm just not sure what I'm going to do there." She then went on to tell me an abridged story of her life – a long procession of travels that astonished me. She hadn't just gone on road trips and bus tours; she'd snorkeled and hiked, she'd tented in the desert. She'd gone by train from Beijing through Manchuria, rode on the Trans Siberian Railroad, and joined hippies travelling in a Ford minivan from Kathmandu to London. To call Olive a traveller would be an understatement.

What did it take, I wondered, to propel a woman on her own to travel the world so extensively? Instinctively, I felt this was too personal a question to ask Olive. As we walked in that warm, moody Miami evening - palm trees deep green and waving above us, I decided to respect the space she had clearly created around herself.

For Olive, Hallmark had been home since 2001. Ever since I'd met her, she was committed to daily walks – several a day, actually - and long walks too. Her walking schedule was predictable, regular, and relentless as the ticking of a clock. I also enjoyed walking in the park behind Hallmark – albeit much less frequently than Olive - and, more often than not on my journeys, her slight and solitary figure would appear in the distance. She leaned slightly – as though if she didn't keep her forward momentum, she'd simply fall over sideways - and walked with a recognizable shuffling gait. It was clear that she loved – needed? - to walk, more than anything else. Movement seemed her one constant companion.

"I've walked three hours today," Olive would say to me as a morning greeting, barely slowing as she breezed by, mopping her brow with a Kleenex. "I must go take a shower." I knew that, after lunch, I'd see her headed out again, her clothes changed, her socks always precisely matching her top. Lime top, lime socks; pink top, pink socks. Olive had an astonishing sock collection.

Snapshot: *We took Aunt Olive to the beach one day. We had parked some distance from the beach, and were walking down a gravel road. She kept wincing, so I asked her what was wrong. She said, "The stones are hurting my feet." I said, "Is there something wrong with your shoes?" and she said, "No." We got to the beach and she took off her shoes. There were great big holes in the soles!*

She asked, "Is it all right for me to walk barefoot?", and I said, "Well, you already are." We walked for a long time - the soles of her feet were like shoe leather - and Olive told us that, when she was a young child on the prairies, she and her brother competed each spring to see how early they could walk barefoot outside. While their Mother would make sure they had their socks and shoes on when they left the house, as soon as they were over the pasture fence, they'd take them off. There was still snow in the corners of the ditches, and they'd be walking barefoot. (Dawna)

Olive was born into the flat, grassy plains of Oak Lake, Manitoba in 1914. She studied teaching in Manitoba, California, and Toronto, and taught in numerous locations around BC and in London, England. While she was in England during the war, Olive met the man she would marry.

Snapshot: *Olive married a Britisher, who'd had children with his first wife. "In times of war, when life is so uncertain, you take love where you find it," said Olive. She loved to travel, but her husband didn't, so they stayed home, except for a short stint in Hawaii. "He was a Brit, so he wanted me to make Yorkshire pudding and all that. Well, I'd never made a Yorkshire pudding, but I had to learn, you know, to please him. After he died, I stopped all that business of cooking. I'd just make myself a salad and then go out and get my main course."* (from Melody's Guatemala journal)

Olive was widowed at 47. Not one to languish in grief, she took up golfing and travelling. She made three trips to Europe, went south to Arizona, taught in Japan, and travelled to Cambodia, returning via the South Pacific Islands. Her next trip was to Cyprus.

After Olive retired from teaching, her travels began in earnest. In Easter of '79, she went by train from Beijing through Manchuria, joined the Trans-Siberian Railroad, and went as far west as Irkutsk. She spent the summer of '79 in China and Korea; in September to December of that same year, 65 year-old Olive travelled from Kathmandu to London, visiting Nepal, India, Pakistan, Iran, Turkey, Greece, Yugoslavia, Italy, Austria, Belgium and England. 'What is enough,

Olive, what is enough?' I wondered as I read through the two-column synopsis of Olive's travels that she had written up. She spent January of 1980 in Israel, and then went home to Canada to rest up…so that, at the age of 67, she could tent in the desert in Egypt. Age 68: Sri Lanka, Burma, Florida. Age 69: Ecuador, Peru, Galapagos Islands. In her 70th year, Olive took a Yangtze River Cruise in China and tacked on travels to Tibet, Japan, Costa Rica, and the Panama Canal. In 1985, Olive chose to spend her 71st year tenting and hiking in Hawaii, snorkeling on the Great Barrier Reef, and exploring in Papua, New Guinea.

Snapshot: *When Aunt Olive went on her trips, she'd lend us her car and we would pick her up when she came back. She was always ready; you never waited for Aunt Olive. One time, we were to take her to the airport for one of her South Seas trips. She stood in the lobby with her purse, a brown overnight bag, and a small suitcase. She was going to be gone for 10 weeks – backpacking in Hawaii, Australia, and snorkeling at the Great Barrier Reef. I said, "You can't be serious! You can't be gone for 10 weeks with two small bags". She said, "Normally I just take one, but my scuba gear is in one of the bags." There was no "I'll miss you," no hugs and kisses, just "bye, see you when I get back." When my husband Jim went to pick her up, he said it was interesting to watch her come off the plane. Aunt Olive was walking head down, until it was like she remembered that someone had come for her, and all of a sudden you could see her eyes* *scanning the crowd. He said, "When her eyes met mine, she broke out in this big smile, as if to say 'there's somebody here - somebody here for me!'" We'd always assumed she was happy in her aloneness, but maybe that wasn't always the case.* (Dawna)

Olive went on to tour New Zealand, and hiked the 53 kilometre Milford Track. In 1987-88, she travelled the game parks of Kenya and Tanzania, and tented and hiked in Zaire, Rwanda, and Uganda. She saw mountain gorillas, and joined a camel caravan in Algeria. She climbed up the Tarsili Escarpment to see prehistoric rock art, and finished off the year relaxing in Texas. In October of 1989, she joined an archaeological trip to the Yucatan, and spent December in Indonesia. Easter 1990 was spent in Guatemala and Honduras, and December in Morocco, where she was mugged in Marrakesh. In 1991, a broken wrist curtailed her travels; Olive travelled only to Ontario. The following year, however, she visited Corsica and Sardinia and, in 1993, went to Jordan, Syria, and Yemen. In 1994, hip trouble curtailed her travels somewhat; her sole trip was to Palm Springs. In 1995, she spent January in South Africa, and October in New England. In 1996, 82 year-old Olive took a Caribbean cruise. And in 1997, she took an Alaskan cruise. Was Olive finally slowing down?

After a car accident in May 2000, Olive moved in with her nephew's family, Jim and Dawna, for a time;

from there, she decided it was time for supportive community living and moved into Hallmark.

When we approached Olive in 2002 to join our pioneering venture to Guatemala, along with staff, owners, and other elders, we knew little of her past travel experience. The trip was motivated by a desire to offer service beyond our building's borders. We were exploring possibilities, and learning as we went. The trip was full of discussion and experience, trial and error. By the end of each day, the richness and intensity of engagement had most of us exhausted. However, unsettling to those of us about half her age, was the fact that 87 year-old Olive – the eldest of the elders travelling with us - put us to bed most nights. We could hear her shuffling around the tiled hotel courtyard afterwards, doing laps late at night. Her unflagging energy was astonishing. Was it restlessness or physical energy, I wondered? Contemplating her continuous movement, I wondered if Olive ever felt like she had arrived.

Meanwhile, the fears Olive had expressed to me before the trip about connecting with younger children proved unfounded. In the orphanage in Antigua, she was seen rocking a baby to sleep with tenderness and ease that befitted the most maternal instinct. Together with all of us, she experienced the power of simple touch and connection. After the trip was over, she repeatedly commented that the most surprising part of the trip for her was to experience the "camaraderie" between the trip members. "In all the trips I've taken," she said, "I've never experienced anything like it."

We were pleased to hear this from Olive. And yet, once we returned to Canada, it was as if the connection on that trip hadn't happened. She would smile pleasantly at my warm greeting, offer a quick hello, and then move on without slowing her pace. Where was the connection we'd made, I wondered, and how did one continue it?

Years later, I asked Dawna my questions. "Where was Olive going?" I asked, as I sometimes wondered if Olive's walking reflected an inner restlessness. "Was she looking for something?" We speculated together as to whether Olive had found refuge somehow in the continual movement of travel. Aware of the inadequacy of our speculations, finally Dawna laughed, "Maybe it's simpler than all that," she said. "Aunt Olive told us repeatedly that she walked for three reasons – to avoid insomnia, obesity and constipation!"

Whatever it was, Dawna had noticed Olive's reticence in her relationships, even though she was socially connected, and a member of several clubs – hiking, walking and bridge. Dawna recalled going to a golf and country club that Olive had been part of, to help her clean out her locker as she was moving to

Abbotsford. "As we walked through the lounge, people wanted to say goodbye to her," said Dawna, "but Aunt Olive just kept on walking, and pushed people's hands away." Was Olive uncomfortable with such open displays of emotion; was she feeling an unwanted weight from the "ties" of relationship?

Who was Olive; what clues has she left behind? Dawna told me that Olive had taken boxes of slides of her first few trips, but after that she'd left the camera at home. "You'd think with all those trips, you'd have reams and reams of pictures, but she didn't." said Dawna. "She was so reluctant to talk – you had to draw each story out yourself because they never came otherwise."

And so, my understanding of Olive remains veiled, lightweight and ever in motion as her carry-on travel bags. A few snapshots, a series of clues. With all the paths Olive wore through the park and on the earth's surface, you'd think that somehow her feet had changed the world, the shape of it – and surely it must have changed her, albeit in ways we'll never know.

Snapshot: *Olive liked to have yogurt with her cereal. She was a woman of habits. At home she'd always had shredded wheat, yogurt and sunflower seeds, so when she came to Hallmark she asked the kitchen staff for yogurt. One of the cooks started putting the yogurt in dishes for her, covered with plastic wrap. Each plastic wrapper was decorated with a drawing or a message -*

a little happy face, or "Good Morning Olive," or "Enjoy your walk today". Olive kept every single one of these wrappers and stuck them to her cupboard doors with scotch tape. After seven years, they faded, but she would not take them down. She told me, "When the cupboard is full, you can take a picture." The wrappers were taken down after Olive passed away. (Dawna)

Today, I'm thinking of Olive, of those plastic wrappers affixed to her cupboard doors – dozens of them; those records – 'snapshots' - of simple daily actions of love that she'd chosen to keep before her. For someone who'd openly disregarded the trappings of the past, it seems a curious action. Over the years, had Olive altered her understanding of what was needed?

I like to think of those plastic wrappers – small, practical, translucent – as clues, small windows into what mattered to Olive - what had always mattered. She had learned to travel light, and certainly had travelled far. And it seems that Olive, inscrutable and dear, in her last days took hold of, and travelled with, the love that had been with her all along

Snapshot: *Shortly after Olive moved to Hallmark and started walking in the park, she said, "There's a fellow in the park who meets me every morning and gives me a hug. He always calls me his dear grandma." I was a little concerned and asked her, "Do you feel threatened by him?" She looked at me as if that was a very strange question and said "No."*

She said, 'Yesterday was New Year's Day and I met my friend there in the park. He asked if he could give me a New Year's Day kiss. And I said, 'Yes, on the cheek'. And he did." (Dawna)

Jake and the squirrel wars

Jake was a package deal: "Love me, love my bird-feeders". He'd brought his own from home, and promptly installed them in Hallmark's back yard. From that day on, Jake was the diligent and committed caregiver for the birds, religiously keeping several feeders topped up. One day, he appeared in my office doorway to inform me that there was a problem with the birdfeeders. "Have we bought the wrong birdseed?" I wanted to know. "Is there a need for more?" "No," Jake had said gravely, "the problem is bigger than that." And, as it turned out, furrier, with more legs. It was the squirrels, Jake told me; the squirrels kept eating the birdseed in the feeders, leaving little for the birds. Jake tried a few deterrents, to no avail. "And then," said Jake, "I tried something different. I took away the wooden pole that held up the bird feeder, because the squirrels were digging their little claws into it, and running right up. I replaced it with a metal pole. Still," continued Jake, looking bewildered, "those rascals keep running up that pole! I don't know how they do it. Any ideas?" he asked. We thought together for a bit, with Jake irritated, and me stifling a grin. Then - Eureka! - I remembered something I'd read somewhere about just such a problem. "Vaseline!" I cried. "Vaseline?" asked Jake, looking even more bewildered. "Yes, Vaseline," I said; "It makes the pole too slippery for any creature to climb, and it doesn't wash off in the rain." Heaven knows, here in BC, you'd need something that didn't wash off in the rain. "Great!" said Jake, and vanished from my office, no doubt, headed for the nearest drugstore.

For the next few weeks, Jake could be seen gazing blissfully out the back windows; the birdfeeders were heaped with seed, and twittering birds of every kind swooped in for the feast. His satisfaction was short-lived. However, it wasn't more than a month later that Jake accosted me as I was walking through Hallmark's front entrance. He took me up to the windows that overlooked the park. "It's not working anymore," said Jake. "It did for a while, but not anymore." "How can that be?" I asked. "How on earth could a squirrel run up what is essentially an oil slick?" "It can't," said Jake, looking miserably out the window. "They aren't climbing the pole. They are climbing the trees beside the feeder, dropping onto its roof, and then eating the seeds." The solution quickly became obvious to us both as we stood gazing at the little house in the woods. Next time I walked past those windows, I saw that the feeder's wooden roof had been replaced by a tin one; it was, I concluded as I watched the roof gleaming moistly in the light, slathered in Vaseline.

I would have loved to have been there to see the first squirrel confidently drop onto that roof! It would be like zip lining without the line...but still, I imagine, with plenty of zip. This solution worked for a time, and I would see Jake complacently smiling at his place in the dining room. Vaseline was here to stay, and all was right with the world.

But then, inexplicably, something changed. Heaven knows what – Jake sure didn't, and I couldn't figure it out either. "It doesn't work anymore," Jake snapped, his irritation thinly-veiled, red creeping up his neck. "That birdseed's disappearing faster than ice in a rainstorm." And it was true. The birdfeed began, once more, to disappear in quantities that our bird population could not possibly consume. Somehow those "crafty little beggars", as Jake called squirrels in his gentler moments, had figured out a way to get past all that Vaseline to their dinner. Jake watched the feeder for hours, but never caught a glimpse of how they did it. Desperately, he began to add contrivances to that feeder as hopeful deterrents: wires and boards and metal pointing in many directions. It began to look like some kind of other-worldly satellite. The birdfeeder became a kind of conversation piece, a point of interest for all walking through our front entrance: "What is *that?*" visitors would ask.

I suppose it would have been easier for Jake to stop stocking that feeder altogether, to just walk away - but he loved seeing the birds, and he was finding it hard to be outsmarted by furry little creatures with much smaller brains. Weeks went by, then months. Eventually the bird feeder stopped changing, stopped morphing into some kind of metal intergalactic space-creature and just sat there as it was: a one-of-a-kind receptacle for squirrel food. Jake had let it go.

Eventually, Jake learned to live in harmony with those wily squirrels, although he could still be heard uttering imprecations under his breath as he regularly dumped large quantities of seed into the Vaseline-laden feeder. He took care, however, not to touch the roof or the pole, for the Vaseline - unlike the birdseed – would not disappear.

Certainly Jake and I feel there is something to be learned from this experience; we're just not sure what.

It'll come to us one of these days.   Perhaps like a squirrel, falling from the sky.

What Anna sees

L ife is bewildering. A whole host of unpredictable factors inform its trajectory. Whatever one believes about the movement of the Divine in the world, it would seem that we're not meant to be wholly protected. An eloquent phrase from the Hebrew Scriptures says that people are "born to trouble like the sparks fly upward." How many times have I sat, fascinated, around a campfire, and watched those sparks against the night sky, glowing red-orange pinpricks of intensity flying in all directions, and vanishing into darkness. Visual chaos, to be sure, and yet, isn't this also what makes the world so beautiful, these sparks, these seemingly capricious moments of the unscripted, the unexpected?

Enter Anna.   Dear Anna, courageous, spirited, self-respecting Anna.   Heartbroken, big-hearted Anna. From the first time I saw her labouring down the hallway on her walker, looking at me with her deep rose-brown eyes, I knew she was a friend.   There was a depth to that brown.   It was a color that I could not describe, which is unusual; I am a painter, and thus have an arsenal of pigment names readily available.   But I had no description for the pigment in Anna's eyes, their hard-won color, warm and lustrous.   I found myself describing it with phrases that weren't visual at all: 'fierce as an eagle, strong as an ox'.   I joined her then, on that icy winter's day as she walked laps up and down the hall. "I was born in Frontier, Saskatchewan," said Anna, "and then we *escaped* the in-laws."   She grinned at me.   "We ended up here in BC, on a berry farm close to the border."   As we neared her suite, she slowed her step and looked over at me.   "But life isn't always happy, you know."

Months later, after our Christmas banquet, I again accompanied Anna up to her room.   I had begun to recognize her as a community-builder.   People were often clustered around her, often in the small seating area beside the laundry room.   Those around her seemed to be quite relaxed - often laughing - and always being very, very honest about things.   And so that December night, as we walked back to her room, I told Anna that I thought she was an amazing person. Anna turned that fierce, penetrating, eagle-eyed gaze toward me and asked why. I told her that it seemed to me that she cared about people and had a good heart, and that this goodness in her drew people together. I said, "You seem uncommonly sensitive to others, so aware of what's around you." She looked at me and said, "You're right about that." Suddenly her face crumpled and her tears flowed freely: "Sometimes I *feel* too much - it is hard." She gathered herself then. "Generally though, I get along just fine. I don't think about that very often."

By this time, we were at her suite entrance. It was festooned with Christmas decorations – red beaded balls hanging from the ceiling and a wreath on the door, all proudly installed by her grandchildren. I took a picture of her that night, in front of her suite door. She was sitting on her walker, resplendent in a blue velveteen top with a shimmering rose-shaped pin, and above it those strong shoulders. Her strong arms were bent across the arms of the walker, and her unflinching eyes were brown as the earth. When I looked at that photo later, I was delighted, for it indeed depicted what I was seeing.

And so I painted Anna. The painting almost painted itself. Her eyes came first, that fierce gaze, and then I worked my way around them, awkwardly as I do when I'm trying to be accurate in angle and line, yet resolute. I worked hard to finish that painting - not to capture Anna, for Anna could not be captured or encompassed, but to allow that gaze to burn through my life and into the world, that gaze that saw things, and that had seen me. I brought the painting to her suite. Anna wept and said, "I'm overwhelmed - I'm looking at *me*. I've had a hard life - so much sorrow and hard work. But I've had much joy too - my children, my friends..."

And then Anna told me the story of her life. She didn't just tell her story, she *spilled* her story, so ripe and ready it was to be told. She spoke of the struggles of poverty in her early years. "Thankfully," Anna said, "though my family was poor and we had to work very hard, it was also a very loving home." As it turned out, Anna had to draw heavily on that love in order to endure the challenges of her next home. "My husband was not always kind," said Anna, her dark eyes smouldering. "I often felt like I was living somebody else's life; I needed to pretend that things were better than they were." For many years, in order to protect herself and her children, Anna had borne her difficulties in silence. She spoke of the way her life changed after her husband died. "Now I can say whatever I want," she said, "I am free to weep or laugh."

She spoke about one of her beloved children who had for years been in the grip of a life-threatening illness. "He's doing okay, though," she said, lacing her fingers together as though in prayer. Anna brightened. "I've had fun too," she said. "I used to dance, used to wish I would die on the dance floor! Waltzing, foxtrot, jitterbug and square-dance – I absolutely loved it. It put me on cloud nine."

Above Anna's couch hung many photos of her family. She gestured toward them, saying, "They give me so much joy! I have many grandchildren and, of course, great-grandchildren," she informed me. "I don't see them very often, but I don't need to." She looked over at me. "Do you know what I mean? she asked. "I love to see them, but I don't *need* to see them. I just need to love them."

Anna's story was one of a woman who had survived and not let go of love. And it was at the intersection of that love and the capricious elements in her story where that irreplaceable, indescribable rich dark brown came to life.

Life is bewildering, and the sparks fly upward, but it is no mystery how it is that Anna still walks, strong and flinty at eighty-eight years of age. It is no mystery that she is still alive, in heart and in spirit. Throughout her life, Anna has chosen the one constant - love - and love, like the brown rich loam of earth, gives life continuously.

And so love is released, while capricious factors flare and burn, sear and blacken. And the sparks and the elements combine; there is combustion. And there is life -

Tea with Marion

I want to tell you about the time I flew," Marion said, "with no help from anyone." With that, she had my full attention, and the attention of everyone else in the room. We were eating lunch together with Hallmark's newest residents, and everyone was swapping stories. Marion went on to tell us about the day when she, as a young girl shaking a small rug out on the back porch, was lifted high into the air by a rogue wind that had roared across the plains. "I was flying!" said the 88-year-old woman, eyes sparkling with triumph and delight. She and her rug were carried some distance before being gently deposited in a neighbour's haystack. She told us that her siblings had tried to repeat the experience, and also that, years later, she and her children would run across the windy Sumas prairie

149

holding a flapping blanket between them. "But nobody else got to fly like I had," said Marion. "To this day, I don't know anyone else who has." She added, with just the flicker of a smile: "I guess they just weren't flying material."

My first trip to her suite soon after was motivated by a desire to record that story, to set it down; it was too magical not to share. What I didn't know was that Marion had taken flight many times since - not in the air, necessarily, but into amazement. It was as if that girlhood experience had opened a window for her, and given her a singular sight and appetite for the mysteries of the natural earth.

And so it was that Marion's door was first opened to me, and during that brief initial tour of the numerous prints and original paintings in her suite, that I saw a lovely ceramic piece of a wee rotund child with arms outspread, and a tiny white and blue bird perched on the child's head. To me it was an eloquent portrait of Marion: a child held in wonder.

From what I could see, Marion was sustained by wonderment. She'd surrounded herself with souvenirs of it; her suite was dotted with caches of unusual fossils and rocks, old Indian beads, and unique artefacts from her travels. Clearly, her relentless curiosity and attentiveness to nature had brought her a continual feast. Even now, from her perch in her suite, her gaze roved to the park outside, mining the movements in the sky and on the ground, constantly wondering at things that most didn't notice.

"Would you like a cup of tea?" she'd asked me on that first day. I'd hesitated. Then, "Sure," I had said, laying aside my list for the day; it was far more interesting to have tea with Marion.

As we waited for the water to boil, Marion showed me a square Chinese ceramic bowl filled with stones. "You don't just get these kinds of stones overnight," she said. And she was right. In raw form, the bowl contained rubies, fools gold, desert roses (fossils), quartz, a petrified cross-section of a tree and numerous other exquisite stones, many of which she knew by their scientific name. I was struck by the variety of textures, shapes and colors; I felt I was looking at a microcosm of the world.

The tea was ready. As I poured milk into mine, Marion spoke about watching eagles and gulls riding the spring wind currents over the small lake outside. "I watched an eagle in the tree over there," she pointed. "He picked off a number of ducklings. One day there were fourteen, the next day there were thirteen, and the next day twelve."

She leaned forward. "I watched the ducks each time it happened; they didn't seem to notice or react.

Do you think they don't care what happens to the other ducks?"

"Maybe they didn't see," said I. "Maybe their little duckling brains aren't developed far enough to recognize what's happening."

"I meant the big ducks," Marion said. "The *big* ducks didn't notice."

"Oh, the *parent* ducks didn't react," I said. "Well…maybe they're trying to keep it together for the sake of the kids." We laughed.

"I often try to understand the violence of nature," I continued. "How can it be so beautiful and so cruel?" I pulled out the small journal that I carry with me all the time, and paged back to notes I'd made during a recent walk. I read it to Marion: *Maybe instead of just random violence and survival of the fittest (although that seems certainly part of it), nature is also a beautiful ground of interdependence and creativity - a rising and falling in which separate beings become part of one another.* "It's kind of like pulling back from whatever's happening in the moment – beautiful, or cruel," I added, "and thinking of it rather as a larger whole, a cycle, or a circle…"

"Does that make sense to you?" I asked Marion, who was leaning forward in her chair, eyes focused with intent as sharp as the rocks tumbled together in her Chinese bowl.

"Does that mean, if I eat you, that I get to be part of the circle?" she quipped. We dissolved into laughter.

"Who gets to eat who first?" asked Marion. "That's what I want to know."

And so began my teas with Marion; there was no allowance for blind romanticism, but lots of room for wonder.

Marion was as aware of propriety as gentry. Once, when our intense conversation about one thing or another was interrupted by the shrill ring of the phone, she exclaimed with irritation "Oh, GO AWAY!" Then, lifting the receiver with her small hand, she said in perfectly modulated tones, rich and silky as cream "Hello. Oh, thank-you so much dear, for phoning!" As she returned the receiver to its cradle, she said, "Oh dear, they seem to think I need reminders to go to lunch. All very well-intentioned, I'm sure, but, where were we?" Neither she nor I could remember.

Marion herself, however, is unforgettable. Her images spill out of her heart fully-formed, ripe like they've been growing for a long time, waiting to be spoken – all her thoughts from over the years, the life lived, the unanswered questions. As the well-schooled speak in complete sentences, Marion speaks in complete stories. I feel I could title each conversation as one would a series of tales, with familiar characters who appear and reappear in each one. "Marion and the

Water Snakes", "Marion Gets a Perm", "Marion and the Green Silk Dressing Gown". Each story emerges complete, with each word placed as flawlessly as a cat's velvet paw along a windowsill, stalking a fly. She lines the basket of each story with beautiful detail, as though inviting all her listeners to curl up with her inside its silken opulence like a litter of kittens. Then there are other, more sombre times, when she'll lead me to a window not yet clear, with only a small opening into that part of her world that is hard to bear, and thus, as yet, unformed.

"I'm coming to grips with living without Phillip. Sixty-five years of marriage is not something you can just chuck," she said one day. "The grief is terrible." We sat, cradling hot cups of tea in our hands; an uncommonly cold snowstorm blustered on the other side of Marion's window. "Phil died in spring." said Marion. "Cancer. We were just about to have a great party. He'd been on medications for over ten years - then it took over, and he was gone in a week." Tears slid down her cheeks; she did not brush them away. "It's terrible that you put grief aside and go on." She told me of numerous travel adventures that she, Phil, and their children had shared in the course of his work as a civil engineer. Abruptly, she turned to address a tiny small movement inside the window at her right. "Now, look at that fly!" she said to me, astonished, and then addressed it directly: "How is it that you're alive?" The fly slowly crawled along the sill, while Marion watched it. "I won't be responsible for your death - you just stay right here where it's warm! I wonder, is it the Buddhists," she asked, "who say that when you die you start all over again, become an insect? Is that Nirvana, do you suppose?" Marion dropped her chin to her chest; her eyes regarded me over her glasses with just a glint of a smile.

"I saw two water snakes once in Sumas Lake," Marion said another time, while looking out of the window; the look in her eyes carried her much further away than that. "They were about this thick" - she made a ring with the tips of her finger and thumb – "and about seven feet long. You could tell they were together by the way they swam." She wove both hands in the air in simultaneous curves.

"I think of my brothers," she said. "We were all just little then." She broke off and leaned towards me. "What is it about us, that we have to kill something just because it's strange?" she asked.

"Somebody killed those water snakes. They chopped them up with a hoe or something. What is it about us?" she asked again, sadly, angrily. There was silence in the room; we looked dumbly out across the shimmering green water of the small lake outside.

One summer afternoon, we brought our cups and cookies to Marion's deck. "Look at the butterflies flying around," said Marion, gesturing towards the deep green lawn below. "I remember one year, when we decided to climb to Crater Lake, and just before we got there, we were enveloped in a cloud of butterflies, and this rustling of wings, and a bitter smell." She stopped, pursing her lips in thought. "Could it have been some kind of repellent, I wonder?" Marion paused for a minute, her pale blue eyes squinting into the sun. "We always had one Monarch flying around all summer at our garden in Vancouver, and at our cabin in Point Roberts too; then one day, it would just disappear."

"Anyway," said Marion, taking another cookie, "years later, I found out that Monarch butterflies fly all the way down to Panama and light on those great big trees. There are so many of them that sometimes they break the trees down. They come from the whole of North America to nest there. Why do you suppose they don't nest here?"

"Looks like this world's not made for efficiency, Marion," I said, grinning. "It's made for wonder."

"Wonder – I like that," said Marion. "Nature – I guess maybe that's God - is such a huge force. The world's been going for a million years, and we've only been here, with the butterflies and animals, for such a short time…" We were quiet for awhile, thinking about it.

"Now, put that together," said Marion suddenly, intensely, "climbing up Crater Lake and having that flock of butterflies over my head, and one of them in each of my own gardens, and then finding out that those ruddy butterflies are flying all the way down to Panama to lay their eggs. It's mind-boggling! *Mind-boggling.*" Marion leaned towards me, brandishing her cookie, "And nobody notices! Probably you and me, and maybe two other people, and it's just this mysterious force. It's scary."

"And that's only the tip of the iceberg, right?" I said. "There's stars and the universe; there's bacteria and plants. And then, there's you and me, Marion, there's *you and me…*!

Marion repeated, "It's scary!" and laughed. "So, what do you do? You eat porridge," she said decisively, settling back in her chair. "I love porridge."

"Me too," I said.

I wondered how, having once flown like that, having seen the world from another vantage point, Marion could so readily touch down, and return to the mundane realm of breakfast oatmeal. I also wondered at the relationship of opposites - at how the mystery of flight for Marion seemed tied so inextricably to mining, to plumbing the everyday, and the earth's often unseen mysteries of rock and dirt and creature.

I have come to see Marion as many things, not the least of which is valiant. Despite the undercurrent of deep, raw grief that runs like a vein through her own earth, she still finds the wherewithal to get up and seek out the wonder of things once again. She continues to dig – more slowly and painfully perhaps – for the hidden gems and artefacts. Marion's gift for flight isn't easy, but it seems to be something she can't stop doing. It's as though it's bred in her bones, that hollowed-out place ever wanting to be filled with wind, wind as essential as breath. So that life won't be so heavy maybe, and so it can be beautiful. So she can (again) have wings.

Agnes and the wild blue yonder

*I*n preparation for our trip to Guatemala, I am with Agnes. At the age of 91, she cultivates a theatrical humour, clapping her hands in delight one minute, and clasping her face in mock anxiety the next. Her angst is not always an act, however, as I soon learn. Though our trip is in two weeks, she seems to feel everything has to be done today, and her anxiety level is high. She trots fretfully, heavily, from one end of her suite to the other as she tells me about the medications she needs to buy, the laundry that must be done. She shows me her travel case stuffed with two pairs of shoes, a nightgown, and some plastic combs. Her passport and medical insurance papers protrude from her purse, and information for a relative is stuffed inside one of its worn leather pockets. "But Agnes," I remind her gently,

"Aren't you supposed to be in the Square in just a few minutes for your Hepatitis booster shot?" Her anxiety flares higher. "I have too much to do," she says, and we go over the preparation list again together - the laundry, the packing, the prescriptions. Then, her smaller concerns crumble to reveal their source: "I'm afraid I'll do something dumb, or hold you all back," she says. "I'm afraid you'll leave me."

I knew Agnes' history; she'd told me her story shortly after she moved in. When she was still young and diagnosed with tuberculosis, her husband dropped her off at the front door of the sanatorium, and she never saw him again. Her two children had died within the next ten years. Agnes surely knows the anguish of feeling unwanted, of being left. Her question leaves me wondering. Over the years, has she come to think of what happened as a result of something she had done? Does she think that it was somehow her fault?

The two of us stand in her rumpled sitting room; clothes are strewn over the chairs and across her bed. I try to reassure her, with a directness that she will understand: "Of *course* you'll do something dumb, Agnes," I say. "We *all* will! And with any luck, we'll get a good laugh out of it. But we will still love you, and we will not leave you." We sit in silence for a minute, contemplating one another. And I wonder what it takes for a woman to survive deep loss, and keep on coming back for more for over ninety years of living. For here was Agnes, despite her fears, choosing yet another new venture as the oldest Hallmark elder to travel to Guatemala. Where did she source her strength, her resilience?

Suddenly, Agnes clasps her hands in front of her, and turns her wrinkled face towards the ceiling. "Oh Lord!" she says (I'm not sure where this is going); "I know that you always love me, but I surely have a hard time believing it. So help me through this day!" And then she is off, out the door, into the wild blue yonder of her life begun again...

Peggy as herself

I think kids are wonderful because they are just themselves," said Peggy, in a statement of such purity that I was rendered momentarily speechless. I had only just approached this former elementary school teacher at her table after lunch, hoping to hear a story or two, and her first, unscripted statement had gone straight to the heart of the beauty of children. How filled with hope that brief phrase, how uncommon that unconditional appreciation for children, who are all too often seen as tiresome – children as interference, children as unwanted work. Here was someone who simply delighted in them. "They don't need your approval for anything," 93-year-old Peggy continued, "especially the mischievous ones."

"I enjoyed the seven year-olds in particular — especially the little boys, who are not scholastic as a rule at that age – they're great," smiled Peggy." My husband used to say after the first day of school, 'Well, which one of the little boys are you going to bring home in your pocket?'"

"I remember one little fellow," Peggy said. "He was a limb of Satan." She laughed at my startled reaction. "My family used that phrase to describe a child with an exceptional sense of humour – which this boy certainly had! If there was a peculiar noise, I knew who it was; I didn't have to turn around. Oh, he was a joy to have around because he was always on the go, but sometimes you wished you could sort of - you know - keep him quiet."

Peggy had been ten years old when her six-year-old brother, whom she adored, became very ill with a ruptured appendix. When gangrene had set in, they'd thought Bill would die. Though he did recover, he contracted smallpox soon after, and was in the hospital for many weeks. "It was his first day back at school after all this," said Peggy. "As usual, I went home for lunch. Bill was already home and very upset. His teacher had strapped him because he had forgotten to bring his reader! Well, I guess I blew up. My mom locked me in the bathroom and, after she thought I was calmed down, she let me out. I went right to school - I can still remember the rage I felt - and after this teacher. But when the principal got hold of me and took me into his office, he was wonderful; he talked to me to try and understand what had happened. He was a good listener, and explained that we didn't behave like that, that we must speak kindly and so on. Anyway, from then on, he and I were pretty good friends. I used to go and visit him, and he'd provide me with reading material, and ask for my thoughts on it." Under his tutelage, Peggy flourished. She had similarly positive connections with her high school teachers. All this cemented her decision to teach, and she chose the primary grades as her forte.

Peggy's first teaching job was in Abbotsford, where she taught six grades in a one-room school. "Thirty-five kids or so, and a stove in the middle of the floor. I was a city girl; I had never had to go out back to go to the bathroom!" She laughed. "I just loved it! My mother couldn't understand this, but it was really a wonderful experience."

What Peggy hadn't realized was that several teachers had already resigned from this particular post, exhausted by the unusually challenging students. "I just walked in to absolute bedlam!" said Peggy. "I thought for sure I'd never be able to teach them. Then one of the older boys said something; I can't remember what it was, but I took exception to it. I pulled him over my knee and walloped his backside with a book! It was more noisy than painful, but apparently it embarrassed him. From that day on, I never had another trouble."

Peggy taught for five years, and then it was wartime. Her beloved younger brother joined the army at 18, and fought in the Battle of Britain. On his 21st birthday, Bill and his fellow RAF fliers were captured by the Japanese in Indonesia; he died in prison. Peggy recalled, "When my mother got word that he had gone, she went to bed that night with her beautiful black curly hair, but when she got up the next morning, there was a streak of white all the way down the middle of her head. It was a tragedy in our family." Peggy paused, and then continued. "I went into the army after that. My fiancé was already overseas, and I followed."

Peggy worked in London for just over four years – of course, in the education section. "I worked at getting training or jobs for Canadian soldiers – sometimes they were recuperating from an injury, and wanting to learn work for when the war was over. Some of them – you'd be surprised at how many – were interested in tapestry and fine needlework; if they were in the hospital, I'd get pictures for them to work on. I enjoyed it, and made a lot of friends."

Peggy married her fiancé after returning home in 1946. "He found a double garage in Abbotsford that had been made into a little house, and we lived in that for a year and a half until we got our place. It was fun.

After our three girls were in school, I went back to teach. I taught for 10 years, and was a school supervisor for 10 more years."

Peggy then told me her favourite story from her years as a supervisor. "One teacher asked each student in her class of seven-year-olds to come with a happy thought to share. So, this little girl came up to tell her happy thought. She stood there and looked at them all and said, 'I think I'm pregnant.' Well, the teacher didn't say anything, and everybody else just nodded. After a while though, the teacher went over to Mary to question her about her happy thought. And Mary explained, 'This morning, Bobby and I were having breakfast, and daddy was feeding the twins, and mommy had the baby. And mommy said to daddy, 'I think I'm pregnant,' and daddy said, 'Now *that's* a happy thought!'"

"One fall, I had about 35 children and, at the end of September, I wanted to do a little report on them - strengths and weaknesses, and so on. Going down my class list, I came to one little lad's name and thought, 'Who is he?' I couldn't place him! I found his desk and looked in it, and not one of his books had been marked by me; he'd obviously never turned a book in, and I'd never noticed. I just was sick about it! The next day, once I had the other kids busy, I went over to his desk. We talked for a minute, and I got down and put my arm 'round him while saying something. He looked at me and said, 'Oh... you *like* me!' And I thought, 'isn't that a terrible thing to be oblivious about one little guy?' He'd just needed a little push to get him going, and did better than I anticipated. After that year, he'd occasionally pop his head in my classroom door to say 'hi'." Peggy thought for a minute, and then said, "He was one of my lessons."

I sat across from Peggy while she told me story after story about the children she'd worked with as a teacher. I drank it all in - there was something I was drinking in alongside them, like sweet milk. It was her clear delight in her students, her gentle tone when speaking of them, the desire she'd had to understand, guide, and support. At one point I found myself saying rather wistfully, "I wish you'd been my teacher." My school experience had its good and bad moments – so what else is new – but the thought of having a teacher who didn't mind, or even *enjoyed*, a child in the margins was compelling. I told Peggy that, while I could still list the names of all my teachers from grade one up to grade eight quite readily, ultimately what I remembered most was whether they liked me or not. And so it is, that teachers leave their imprints on our lives as surely as a hand on wet sand.

Who would we be if we felt truly loved, I wondered, and how different would that person be than who we've become over the years? Why is it, all too often, that we think we need to become someone else in order to be worthy of love?

As I've aged, I've longed for that simplicity, that unapologetic purity of being true to myself. I don't know why 'being yourself' often seems like a foreign land, I don't know why the road to that place feels long and obscure. You'd think it would be the easiest thing in the world.

"Do you think it's possible, later in life, to return to that state of being 'just ourselves?'?" I asked Peggy. "Can we find that place again, or is it irretrievably lost?"

Peggy was quiet for a moment, toying with her coffee cup. "I think you build on it; you get more wisdom, grow more tolerant. When I was growing up, my father had a very good job. We had a fridge when most had an icebox, and while we weren't rich, we were comfortable, and my parents wanted the best for us. When I joined the army, I found there were other kinds of people. At first, I was kind of shocked - their language and ways were so different – and then I found that many of them were wonderful, and my outlook changed. So, I think the best of you can come out as you grow older. You've got more time to relax; I find myself enjoying things like reading now, without worrying if I'm wasting time. And so, hopefully, over the years, we develop, and can become ourselves as we were meant to be."

Our conversation ended. I went for a walk up the side of a mountain, and sat on a rock overlooking the Fraser Valley, its postage stamp lots and fields dotted with life, cars crawling in the distance. And here I was, having crawled up here myself, trying to figure out what Peggy's stories, fraught with love, had to say; there was some vital undercurrent beneath them all.

We begin our lives in that purest of places, our true selves; it is there that we are met by our teachers, our family, the world. Are we utterly and inevitably formed in our early years, by those who love and praise us, or by those who disapprove and glower? Or might it be, as Peggy suggests, that we can grow into ourselves as we age, almost like a second chance? And who is my teacher when, in middle age, I sit atop a mountainside and take stock?

My thoughts returned to what Peggy had said at the beginning of the visit; I realized that her expansive opening statement also included her own self. For Peggy was being her true self by loving children for being themselves. Maybe if we spent as much time trying to love as to *be* loved, we wouldn't wander so far away from who we are.

The late afternoon sun began to fade into coolness, and I reluctantly stood up from my perch on the rocks to return home. As my feet automatically followed the path that wound its way down the slope, my thoughts began to untangle, and resolve into quiet.

When we are young, we see ourselves held in the eyes of others and measured there. When we are older, maybe we are the ones looking with measured gaze into the mirror – not only asking 'who am I', but hopefully also believing that, no matter how murky the reflection, there is someone worth saving.

If good teachers – true teachers – remind us of who we are, and in our adult years, that role transfers onto our own shoulders, then it is ours to do the work of remembering, and staying true to the path that's been given us, that has always been there. I like Peggy's take on it, that being oneself is something to relax into, and build upon. Perhaps among the rewards would be a freedom and peace in old age – or maybe at any age. Peggy learned this, it seems, a long time ago, when she opened her arms to all those children.

Threading the needle

When Norm made the decision to move into Hallmark, he was finding it difficult to adjust to dramatic changes in his life. He had been a powerful and active man in his community - a School District Administrator, soloist, choir director and father - until his life took several sharp turns. Close on the heels of his early retirement, his wife had died, and shortly afterwards, Norm was diagnosed with Parkinson's.

Thankfully, our community setting improved his health and spirits, and Norm agreed to lead a bimonthly hymn sing. On a good day, he was a skilled and joyful song leader. On a bad day, Norm didn't want to leave his room. He could not control the shaking in his hands; he did not want to be seen.

Norm was part serious, part playful. While you knew just looking at him that he had worked in positions of authority, he was just as willing, with a boyish grin, to share his 'joke of the day'. He'd disappear into the Hallmark workshop for hours at a time, crafting wooden games with a hidden trick to them, a pastime which also gave him great amusement.

Norm was not afraid of risk. He'd told me, with a twinkle in his eye, of the January choir practise he had attended as a young man, where he'd first glimpsed his future wife Mary. He'd bided his time - well, sort of. He did wait until May for their first date, but proposed to her before the evening was over! They were married three months later, and many good years ensued.

Norm had lived at Hallmark for several years when we approached him with our own audacious proposal. Stan, an owner of Hallmark, had come up with a crazy idea. Believing that a healthy community needed engagement beyond its own borders, he suggested we explore service trips to Guatemala. Stan's idea was that both Hallmark residents and staff should be invited to participate. Our conversation with Norm went something like this:

"Hey Norm, what are you doing next spring?"

"I don't know; why?"

"Would you like to travel to Guatemala with us?"

(Pregnant pause)

"To Guatemala?"

"Yup."

"Why Guatemala?"

"Well, we're exploring ways that our Hallmark community can engage beyond its own borders, and we've found an orphanage in Antigua that's open to our involvement."

Norm's eyes filled with tears. "Did you know that my wife and I had a lifelong dream of going to Central America together?" he asked.

Norm told us he'd taken early retirement so they could fulfill their dream. However, Mary's arthritis worsened, and she became housebound. Norm served as her primary caregiver until she died of cancer six years later; the loss he felt was acute. This, coupled with the diagnosis of Parkinson's had led him to put that dream away, calling it his "lost dream of international service".

"I can't always button up my clothes in the morning," said Norm then. "And I can't handle heat."

Stan asked, "What if you roomed with Allan? He could help you get dressed if you need it. And it's not that hot in Antigua in April...."

Norm drew his coffee cup towards him for one last swig. "Do you really think I could do it?"

"We're willing to try if you are, Norm," said Stan; his face showed both uncertainty and resolve. "Why don't you talk with your family, and think about it for a while?"

And so, Norm flew with us to Guatemala that spring, and spent 10 days sharing what he had to give. One of our favourite photographs from that trip still hangs on the wall at Hallmark. It's of Norm sitting in a rocking chair in the orphanage, with a baby in his arms. Norm's first comment when he saw us hanging the picture was "I want you to know that I put that baby to sleep! The baby in the picture is still crying."

Someone had sewed brightly coloured kite pillows for us to give away in Guatemala. They were about the size of teddy bears and were meant for people in the orphanage's post-op, to cheer up their room. We had packed them unstuffed, and therefore, one afternoon were all in the hotel sitting room stuffing the kites and sewing the edges together. Stan was having trouble threading his needle. Norm, who'd been standing over by the window where the light was best, said, "I'll thread it for you!" Stan laughed. "Yeah, right - a guy with Parkinson's is going to thread this needle!" Norm laughed right back and waved him over. We all stopped to watch as Norm held Stan's needle and thread up to the light. Whammo, first try, right through the center! For the remainder of the trip, Norm made good use of that moment. "Need help with anything, Stan?" he'd say with a grin, "Anything at all?"

Upon his return, Norm told a local newspaper reporter, "I went to Guatemala to challenge a handicap that I have – Parkinson's. And I learned to focus on what I *could* do, rather than what I couldn't do." While Norm was more and more affected by his condition over time, his spirit seemed only to strengthen. The following summer, just over a year after his Guatemala trip, Norm came down the hall toward me, waving a certificate over his head. "What's that, Norm?" I asked. "Oh, it's just a little information about something I did with my grandson last week." It was, in fact, a certified statement that Norm had gone white-water rafting.

Why stop there? It seemed that once he'd cleared the hurdle of his Parkinson's, the world was once again Norm's playground. And so it was, in the last years of his life, Norm chose to re-enter one of the greater, more vulnerable risks of life. He fell in love again.

....

Pink fingernails, pink lipstick, pink cowboy hat, casinos and laughter. That was Joan. Tall, distinguished administrator and church choir director, avid collector of mechanical train sets and bolero ties; a prairie boy all the way. That was Norm.

An unlikely pairing, to be sure. But, without a doubt, Norm had fallen head over heels in love with a woman as vivid and full of life as he was. Despite his Parkinson's, despite their ages, despite - no doubt - other obstacles that we knew nothing about, Norm and Joan were risk-takers par excellence.

Norm told me bits of their story one day, how he had stood up in the Dining Room and asked anyone wanting to be part of a regular Scrabble group to come see him after the meal. Joan, all smiles, had approached him. Once they'd set the time and day for their first game, she'd flashed him a smile, stood on her tiptoes, and planted one fine pink-lipsticked kiss on his cheek. From that moment on, Norm was besotted.

It became a common sight to see Norm and Joan together over a Scrabble game, or lingering over a cup of coffee after a meal. The ensuing years weren't easy – Parkinson's was a roller-coaster ride, and an unpredictable one at that. "I walk a lonely road," Norm said to one of the staff on a particularly difficult day. Still, in the midst of it all, Joan and Norm seemed inseparable. We were glad they had each other.

It was a courageous love, for both of them. When Joan became ill, Norm remained a faithful companion. "I told her I'd never leave her, and I didn't," Norm told me while Hallmark staff set up the chairs for Joan's memorial. "She was in my arms when she took her last breath." I wondered at Norm at that service, as he gallantly handed each woman coming into the service a bright pink rose – Joan's favourite. At how he sat in the front row with her family, his companionship with Joan honoured; how he sang the hymns with heartfelt conviction, and despite this most recent loss, seemed suffused with peace.

I'd met Norm in the hallway a few days earlier, and heard what his doctor had told him at a recent visit: "You've got 15 more years in you, Norm." Norm had replied, "Extend it by another five, and I'll go for 100 years old!" And so, a few weeks later, when Norm fell ill and was taken to hospital, we expected a short stay. We were shocked when we heard that Norm had died.

For days afterward, the community was in disbelief. Norm had died within a few weeks of Joan's death. A broken heart? Coincidence? Who can say? All we knew was that Norm and Joan together had brought forth a beauty, and had given themselves valiantly to life.

From what I could see, Norm and Joan had threaded the needle's narrow eye of their later years right through its center.

We were left holding that bright pink rose – that memory of him and Joan - cherished, in a vase. Reminding us of the beauty and richness of life that is here for the taking, despite obstacles, despite suffering. It reminds us of what beauty can unfold when we're open.

Notes

2. Introduction

    1.   (From *The Active Life* by Parker J. Palmer, 1990, Harper and Row, San Francisco, p. 98.)

13. Tim in the sun

    1. (*Leisure*, by William Henry Davies)

16. Mary at the elevator

    1. ("Hawking concedes black hole bet", Jenny Hogan, Dublin. Article, *Newscientest* 21 July 2004.)

18. Elaine and the golden years

    1. (*Thanatopsis*, by William Cullen Bryant)

Thanks and acknowledgements

To my family who keep their doors and hearts open to me whenever I come home. A specific mention (or two): To mom and dad who thought the book was wonderful even before they'd read a word. To Bonnie, who got all jazzed with me when the title *finally* arrived. And to Roger, for listening.

To those who walk closest these days, my dear kindred companions, especially Anne, Andrea, Bev, Dorothy, Deb, Heidy, Joyce, Sharon...where to start, when to end? Your presence in my life is essential and life-giving. These days I'm more aware than ever that a book – a life - is a work of community, and am grateful to these and many others who've walked with me along the way.

*T*o Hallmark staff, who help keep the boat afloat, and know many more of our elder's stories than I ever will. To friends and family members, who filled in the spaces for some stories. And to Linda and all of Hallmark's community members for keeping on keeping on working for the good.

*T*o those who offered gentle feedback and solace when I needed it. And to those who did the rigorous work of editing, especially Andrea and Dave.

*T*o Stan and Grace, whose shared vision for a continuously evolving creative community has not only birthed and tangibly sustained the work of these writings, it has fostered a receptive ground from which hopefulness and vitality can grow.

*T*o the Unnameable One, who calls me into the heart of story, and speaks continually of belovedness.

*T*o each Hallmark elder whose stories – told or untold here – are a gift. Some appear in this book, and others are held in my heart. Your trust is precious, your open door an honour.

*T*o *all* well-aged elders, here and passed. Your stories help us uncover our own. And to all who pick up this book and read these stories, or sit at the feet of your own well-aged elders, may it be so for you...

I read somewhere that, like a child in a sandbox, a writer must have the freedom first to make a mess, and out of that mess a sandcastle. I am quite adept at the mess part! The sandcastle emerged with the help and insight of my hardworking editors. Andrea weathered my first draft valiantly, and worked hard to get inside my head. She also knew when to get out - when the walls were crumbling - and helped shore them up! After her edits, my sandcastle stood stronger, with clearer lines. I know the editing time took her away from tending her own gardens (metaphorical and real), and am deeply grateful for her heart, work and contribution. Next, Dave came in and helped carve further, until the stories I had hoped to tell stood out in sharp relief. He too brought heart and insight to the process. And to Stan, "co-investor" from the first shovelful of sand to the final edifice, who continually encourages me to trust my own voice, and "take the risks you feel may be worth it". I am blessed to have such wonderful companions in the sandbox.

And finally, to everyone who I've failed to mention here, and will no doubt only remember this – horrified - *after* this work has gone to print. You are truly valued even though my sputtering memory, like my old Volvo, just doesn't always make it up the hill...

About the Author

*M*elody Goetz was born in Saskatchewan, and has spent much of her life on the Canadian prairies. She graduated with a Bachelor of Fine Arts (Major: painting) from the University of Manitoba in the late '80's. She's settled into naming meaningful work and communications as her polestar, and is a practicing painter and writer. Her first poetry chapbook, *train to Mombasa* (a long poem set in Africa) was published in 2000 (Punchpenny Press). Her short fiction and poetry has appeared in numerous Canadian periodicals and anthologies. She now lives in BC's Fraser Valley, where she works in senior management for Hallmark Communities, Inc., and hikes into the deep green forests of British Columbia's coastal mountains every chance she gets.